The POWER of POSITIVE CONFESSION

Develop a Habit of Speaking Life,

Not Death!

by

Frederick K.C. Price

FAITH ONE
PUBLISHING

LOS ANGELES, CALIFORNIA

The Power of Positive Confession
Develop a Habit of Speaking Life, Not Death!
Revised & Expanded
formerly known as
Name It and Claim It!
ISBN 10: 1-883798-61-2
ISBN 13: 978-1-883798-61-1
Copyright © 1992 by
Frederick K.C. Price.
P.O. Box 90000,
Los Angeles, CA 90009

Published by
Faith One Publishing
7901 South Vermont Avenue
Los Angeles, California 90044

TABLE OF CONTENTS

INTRODUCTION

Proverbs 18:21:

Death and life are in the power of

the tongue, and those who love it

will eat its fruit.

Proverbs 18:21 tells me that with my tongue I can speak *death* to my life and I can speak *life* to my life. My life then is controlled by my tongue. *Death and life, life and death are in the power of the tongue.*

This principle of death and life being in the power of the tongue, I call "the power of positive confession."

Since I will be using it in this book frequently, let me define the word *confession* so that we will be on one accord. But first, I want to ask you a question and I want you to be honest about the answer:

What is the first thing that comes to your mind as you read the words, *The Power of Positive Confession*? You probably thought about a negative, right?

If you ask the average person, in 99.9% of the cases, you will find that the word *confession* is always associated with a negative, usually sin. It is usually thought of in the context of "Father, forgive me. I blew it. I messed up. I did something wrong." This is our normal thinking about the word *confession*. In other words, there is more said in the average church about a negative confession than there is about a positive confession. In fact, from childhood, we are conditioned to the negative, more than we are to the positive. This idea of negative rather than positive associated with the word *confession* is instilled in our children.

We, as the children of God, however, need to recognize that there is more in the Bible about a positive confession than there is about a negative confession.

Now, to our definition: The Greek word for *confession* is *homologeo*, and it means "to agree with" or "say the same thing that God says about you and or your circumstances." It does not mean, per se, to confess a negative. Most of the time, however, we are confessing something bad, something negative, something that we have done wrong.

Do not misunderstand me, though. If you have done something wrong, you ought to confess it. But we should not spend our whole life confessing wrong. We ought to be living in such a way that there is very little that we should have to confess.

In this book, my desire is to share with you what I believe God means by confession, what the Word says about confession, and how what you say or confess with your tongue can affect every aspect of your life. I trust you will learn that through your confession, you will add life to your life, or death to your life. My desire is that you begin to speak *life* to your life.

CHAPTER ONE

POSITIVE CONFESSION; POSITIVE THINKING

Proverbs 18:21 is the biblical foundation for the principle of death and life being in the power of the tongue. I call this life-and-death principle "the power of positive confession." What principle could be more powerful and more vital to the people of God?

The primary thing that we do with our tongue is speak or talk. We would have a very difficult time talking or verbalizing without a tongue. Yes, it is true that we use our tongue to eat and that our taste buds are located on our tongue, but generally, we talk more than we eat. Or we should.

You have a real problem if you eat more than you talk. And, maybe that is the problem with some people. Christianity is actually a confession, from the beginning to the end, whether we like it or not. And, true Christianity is a positive confession. I did not say true Christianity was positive thinking, although positive thinking can play a role in our positive confessions.

Some years ago, there was a book written by Norman Vincent Peale, which was a best-seller all over the world. It was titled, *The Power of Positive Thinking.* I submit to you that it is certainly good to think positively. There is no question that you will be better off in life if you learn to think positively. But I believe that positive thinking is only the first stage of something bigger. If positive thinking is all you're ever exposed to, that is well and good because that is better than being exposed only to negative thinking. However, if all you ever do is *think* positively, you will never learn how to *speak* positively.

You must start out from a premise of positive thinking. But if all you do is think positively and never move into the next stage, then you will stay—as far as your circumstances are concerned—in the same environment. All that will happen is that you will have a better attitude. You will be able to smile while the ship is sinking, instead of wringing your hands, crying, screaming and hollering.

However, if you learn to *speak* positively based on the Word of God, you can keep the ship afloat! And, that is the major difference.

Thinking positively instead of negatively is better; there is no question about that. However, we want to go on to God's best. Positive thinking is absolutely correct. It is right. It is proper. It is good, and that is where we start, but that is not where we end. If you only think positively, all you will do is affect your attitude about your circumstances, but you will not change them. When they amputate your leg, because of positive thinking, you will be able to accept it by rationalizing, "Thank God I'm not dead. Thank God I didn't go to the cemetery. I'll be limited in what I can do, but thank God, I'm not dead." You will affect yourself in that way, but I believe that if you learn the principle of positive confession, you can change your circumstances, and that is what is important.

WHAT IS CONFESSION?

Confession in the Greek language means that you "agree with" or "say the same thing that God says about you and or your circumstances." Do you realize that the only way you can get saved is by confession? "Oh, no, Brother Price, you don't get saved by confession, you get saved by believing." That is partially true; believing is involved, but if you do not confess what you believe, you still will not get saved. That statement may not be denominational or theological, but it is biblical.

Salvation involves confession and has nothing to do with emotions. Yet, in most cases, Christians have been guided toward emotion rather than confession.

In most churches, we are usually told that if we confess our sins the Lord will save us, and that is untrue. That is not the way you get saved. Nowhere in God's Word does He require the sinner to confess his sins, so that he can get saved. This is not taught in the Bible. It is taught in certain ministry classes in some churches. It is taught in certain kinds of evangelistic outreaches. It is taught in certain Sunday School quarterlies, but it is not taught in the Bible.

You ought to thank God that He does not require you to confess your sins in order to get saved, because if He did, then you would have to confess every one of them in order to get saved. You could not leave one out because the concept is not to confess some of your sins, but to confess your sin(s). That is plural. That means every one. It is just like dialing a telephone number. There are seven numbers, and if you leave one of the numbers out, you do not get the party you are calling. It is like a combination lock: If you leave one of the numbers out, you do not open the lock.

Let me say this to you, so that you will get it straight for the rest of your life. When you glibly say, "Lord, forgive me of my sins," that amounts to nothing at all. "Forgive me of my sins." What sins? Which ones do you need to be forgiven of? I do not need to be forgiven of the sin of adultery, because I have never committed that sin. So, why include that in my prayer? I must specify what I want to be forgiven of.

I should be confessing what I have sinned, so that I can be forgiven of the sin. So, to say, "Lord, forgive me of my sins," is not biblical. I know it is traditional—people do it all the time, but that is not why the person got saved.

Nowhere in the Bible does God require the sinner to confess his sins in order to get saved. I know there is a verse in 1 John 1:9, which says: *If we confess our sins, He is faithful and just to forgive us our sins and to cleanse us from all unrighteousness.* That verse has been taken out of its setting and applied to sinners, although it is not even for sinners. John was not writing to sinners, he was writing to Christians. He said, *My little children. . . .* We have taken that verse out of its setting and used it as a ministering tool for sinners, saying, "If you confess your sins, God will forgive you." No! You may go through all of that, but that is not why God forgave you.

The fact is, God really does not actually forgive the sinner's sins in order to be in a position to save the sinner. In a very broad sense, yes, God forgives the sinner's sins, but that is not really what salvation is based on.

What God actually does with the sinner's sins is to remit them. The Apostle Peter began that message on the day of Pentecost (Acts 2:38). He said, *Repent, and let every one of you be baptized in the name of Jesus Christ for the remission* [not for the forgiveness] *of sins; and you shall receive the gift of the Holy Spirit.*

Remission means to send it away from you. You receive a bill from the department store or wherever, and it says, "Please enclose this stub with your remittance." Your remittance is something you are going to send away from you. What God does is send the sinner's sin away from him. He really does not forgive it. He remits it. He treats it as though it never was! Technically, the only sins that God forgives are Christians' sins.

There is a confession that the sinner must make in order to get saved, but it is not a confession of sin.

Let me say it again: Christianity is a confession, but not a confession of sin. God does not require sinners to confess their sins in order to get saved. First John 1:9 is not for sinners. Technically, it is for Christians. Let us look at that scripture more closely.

*If we confess our sins, He is faithful
and just to forgive us our sins and to
cleanse us from all unrighteousness.*

Unrighteousness is the word *righteousness* with the prefix "un," which means "non-righteous." The scripture says, *If we confess our sins* [s-i-n-s], *He is faithful and just to forgive us our sins and to cleanse us from all unrighteousness.*

Question: What do you normally clean up? You usually clean something that is dirty. But wait a minute! What can get dirty? Something that is *already* clean. If there was never any clean, there could not be any dirty. So, cleanse implies dirty.

Cleanse us from all unrighteousness would imply that the individual who is confessing his sins was once righteous. He sinned and the sin dirtied his righteousness, and the end result was unrighteousness. If you confess your sins, God will clean you up and wash away the dirty, and when you wash away the dirty, you do away with the "un" and you have "righteousness" left. Obviously the unrighteousness was first of all righteousness.

That could not be talking about sinners, because they have never been righteous. You cannot be righteous unless you are born-again, unless you are a child of God, having accepted Jesus as your personal Savior and Lord.

Second Corinthians 5:21 informs us that *He made Him who knew no sin to be sin for us, that we might become the righteousness of God in Him.* By accepting Jesus as your personal Savior and Lord, you become a righteous person. Sinners never had any righteousness, so they could never be cleaned up from it.

Christians have or are "righteousness," but we can sin. When we sin, it is really not that we lose our righteousness, but we lose our sense or consciousness of righteousness, and we do not "feel" righteous anymore.

You lose your sense of righteousness, but you do not lose your righteousness (which means right-standing with God), any more than your child loses you as the mother or the father, just because he went into that cookie jar and took those chocolate chip cookies when you told him not to. He took the cookies and you may have to correct him, but he is still your child. I do not care what that boy does, that is still your child. He can go to court and have his name legally changed, but it does not change the fact that he is still your child.

WHAT MUST THE SINNER DO ABOUT HIS SIN?

If you birthed that child, there is nothing anybody in this world can do to change it. Changing your name does not change your birth. So if you are a child of God when you sin, you do not lose your *sonship* or relationship, but you break your fellowship. Sin breaks fellowship.

I want to say it again: I John 1:9 is for Christians, not for sinners. If I John 1:9 is not for sinners, what is the sinner supposed to do about his sins? REPENT! FORSAKE THEM! STOP! in the name of the Law of God. The sinner is supposed to confess Romans 10:9-10:

9   *that if you confess with your mouth the Lord*
     Jesus and believe in your heart that God has
     raised Him from the dead, you will be saved.

10   *For with the heart one believes unto righteousness*
     and with the mouth confession is made unto
     salvation.

Notice that salvation comes by your mouth, not by confessing sins, but by confessing Jesus. Christianity is confession from beginning to end. You confess your way into the Kingdom of God with your mouth, and then you confess your way to the top of righteousness and victorious living in Christ.

NEVER GIVE UP SAYING AND BELIEVING

Matthew 10:32-33: Jesus is speaking—think of it in reference to confession:

32   *"Therefore whoever* [what?] *confesses Me before*
     men [that means in front of men because God
     does not have any secret disciples], *him I will*
     also confess before My Father who is in heaven.
     [In other words, if you talk about Me
     unashamedly in front of men, I will talk about
     you unashamedly in front of My heavenly
     Father.]

33   *"But whoever denies Me before men, him I will*
     also deny before My Father who is in heaven.

We read in Proverbs that death and life are in the power of the tongue. Now look at John 12:42-43:

42   *Nevertheless even among the rulers many believed in Him, but because of the Pharisees they did not confess Him, lest they should be put out of the synagogue;*

43   *for they loved the praise of men more than the praise of God.*

There is a price to pay to make a positive confession in line with the Word of God. Hebrews 10:23 says, **Let us hold fast the confession of our hope without wavering, for He who promised is faithful.** This scripture tells us to hold fast the confession of our hope or, in others words, faith without wavering; (for He is faithful that promised). In other words, do not give up saying and believing. I added *believing* because believing goes with faith.

Never give up saying what you hope or have faith for. Do you have a hope that is consistent with God's plan and purpose? If so, keep saying it. Hebrews 10:35-36 say:

35   *Therefore do not cast away your confidence, which has great reward.*

36   *For you have need of endurance, so that after you have done the will of God, you may receive the promise:*

Now what is your confidence? Your confidence is your hope spoken of in the 23rd verse of Hebrews 10. And, what is your hope? Your hope is in what God said in His Word, and the Bible says that God's Word is forever settled in heaven. The Bible says that not one jot or tittle will fall from God's Word until all be fulfilled.

You can count on whatever you base your hope on, that is in line with God's Word, so hold fast to that. What is the will of God? The will of God is whatever God tells you to do in reference to what it is you are believing God for.

You have to find scripture and then whatever that scripture tells you, hold on to that. For example, let us say that a husband and wife want to get into agreement and believe God for a certain thing. They want to pool their faith, or put it together. They would use a scripture like Matthew 18:19 *that if two of you agree on earth concerning anything that they ask, it will be done for them by My Father in heaven.* This scripture is the will of God for more than one person who wants to get in agreement with another person. Do not cast that away.

CHAPTER TWO

YOU WILL HAVE
WHATEVER YOU SAY

W e will look at another verse of scripture that deals with confession, and then I will show you how to determine the will of God.

Mark 11:23, Jesus is speaking:

> "For assuredly, I say to you, whoever says to this
> mountain, 'Be removed and be cast into the sea,'
> and does not doubt in his heart, but believes that
> those things he says will be done, he will have
> whatever he says."

Confession is saying, and saying is confession. Now your heart is your spirit, that is your inner man. That is the *real* you. Notice that in Mark 11:23 when the word *believe* is used the second time, the word *heart* is not mentioned with it. It is obvious that if He does not want you to doubt in the heart, He must want you to do the believing in the same place where He does not want the doubt.

As a result, I think it is a safe assumption — and that we do no injustice to the scripture to paraphrase it and say it this way: . . . *and does not doubt in his heart, but will believe in his heart*. . . . Can you see that? Doubt is the opposite of believing. If you are believing, you are not doubting; if you are doubting, you are not believing.

Notice again, He says, *but believes that those things he says* [confession] *will be done, he will have whatever he says* [confession]. They have not come to pass yet, because if they had already come to pass, you would not have to say it, because you would have it. *Will be done* is future tense — future to the saying of it, future to the believing of it in your heart. If you already had it, you would not have to believe it. This is the rule. This is the will of God.

WHAT IS THE WILL OF GOD?

The will of God is that you have to say it with your mouth and you have to believe it in your heart without any doubt. As a result, Jesus said . . . *he will have whatever he says* . . . . He did not say you will have whatever you need; He said you will have whatever you say. We must be careful here, because Jesus is enunciating a divine, universal law. We must remember that laws can work for you, but the same law can also work against you if you do not observe the conditions that cause the law to operate.

If I plug my television into the electrical outlet, I can watch the "Ever Increasing Faith" TV program and be ministered to. However, if I take my fingers and wet them and stick them into the wall socket, that same electricity that will allow me to watch *Ever Increasing*

Faith will also allow me to ever increasingly die! I would not be observing the law.

If you form the habit of saying negative things, even jokingly, then where do you separate the joke from the reality? When does it get to the point where you are really "saying" out of your heart? Because you have formed the habit of saying negative things so much, after a while, you begin to apply that negativism to the positive things that you want to say, and you will end up getting the wrong thing.

Think about this, because most of us have done it: You go to the restaurant, the waiter or waitress comes over, hands you the menu and asks if anybody wants anything to drink—cocktail or whatever. They do not know who you are, so they assume that you want something to drink. You might say, yes, coffee, Coke, or something like that. Then he or she might say, "I'll give you a little time to look at the menu." You then select what you want from the menu. The waiter or waitress then returns and says, "Are you ready to order?" "Yes, I believe I will have the chicken fricassee." Or, "Yes, I believe I will have shrimp scampi."

"I believe I will have . . . I believe. . . ." Come on! You don't believe it; you are going to have it. That is what you want. "I will have," or, "I think I'll try. . . ." You are not going to try it; you are going to order it, and eat it. Is that not right? I want shrimp scampi, and I intend to eat shrimp scampi until the eating tells me I do not like it. Then the eating will stop on scampi and I will order something else, or I will not come back to that restaurant anymore.

Consider Mark 11:23: If all you do is believe you will have scampi, you will never get it. You will have to say it. You will have to confess it to the waiter or the waitress or you will not get it. They will not allow you into the kitchen to cook you own food at the restaurant!

For assuredly, I say to you, whoever says . . . . With this verse, Jesus is enunciating a law, and as amazing as it may sound, this law will work for sinners as well as it will for Christians. The difference is that for the non-Christians, there is no life in it, but it will still work.

Two plus two is four whether you are a sinner or a Christian because that is a mathematical law. It is a principle. If the worst person in the world adds up a column of figures, 2 plus 2 will still equal 4, because that is a principle.

DEVELOP A HABIT OF SPEAKING POSITIVELY

Christians need to learn how to be positive. By this I mean positive in line with God's plan and purpose. I am not talking about the power of positive thinking as some kind of esoteric regimen. That is good, but it is not good enough for us to achieve what God would have us to achieve.

This is the point I want to make. Thinking positively is always better than thinking negatively, and it will put you in a better frame of mind to accept what is going on around you. However, it will not change your circumstances. On the other hand, the power of positive confession, in line with God's Word will change your circumstances in a positive way.

Jesus said, in Mark 11:23:

> For assuredly, I say to you, whoever says to this mountain, "Be removed and be cast into the sea," and does not doubt in his heart, but believes that those things he says will be done, he will have whatever he says.

That means you will have the negative as well as the positive. If you do not want the negative, you had better stop saying the negative.

Why not say something that will help reinforce in you positive ideas so that you develop them into habits? When you get to a situation in life, you don't have to say, "What shall I say now?" You don't want to say "Take care." You don't want to say "She makes me sick." When you develop a habit of speaking positively, you will not have to say that, because it will become easy, an automatic reflex action. According to Mark 11:23, the will of God is for us to say it with our mouths and believe it in our hearts.

I want to show you a mathematical equation so that you will understand how important the things I have stated are. If the number of times a thing is repeated is any indication of its importance, then we need to be very careful that we learn the lessons that the Spirit of God is showing us in the Word of God. As we read Mark 11:23 again, I will point out this mathematical equation:

> For assuredly, I say to you, whoever (1) **says** to this mountain, 'Be removed and be cast into the sea,' and does not doubt in his heart, but (1) believes that those things he (2) **says** will be done, he will have whatever he (3) **says**.

Notice the ratio, 3 to 1. Jesus only mentions *believing* one time, but He mentions *says* three times. I wonder if the Man is trying to tell us something? Yes! He knew that Christians would not have a problem with the believing part because they will believe anything, even a lie.

People do not have a problem with believing. However, where they fall short is "saying." "Honey, you ain't gonna get me to say that! I ain't gonna say that I got something I can't see. You ain't gonna make a fool out of me."

Jesus knew that people would not have a problem believing. Their problem would be confessing or saying. Inhibitions, self-centeredness, not wanting to look different to other people are problems for most people. Now, we will dress like a fool and look different, but for some reason, that does not bother us. However, when it comes to saying something that lines up with the Word of God that is a problem. When it comes to the things of God, most people suddenly have this great spirit of sincerity rising up in them. This great "honesty" spirit comes on them, and this great desire to be perfectly circumspect.

Yet, oftentimes they say they have things that they do not have and never think anything about it.

Here's an example:

"Say man, I haven't seen you in a long time. When are you going to give me my five dollars you told me you were going to give me three weeks ago?"

"See me Friday I'll have some money then."

You are telling a lie. Friday has not come yet. The company you work for may go bankrupt and if it does you will not have any money on Friday. However, you are already confessing the future, and you have no problem with that.

"Meet me right here outside the gate, and I will have my paycheck on Friday."

We do not have a problem with that because we believe the word of men. The man told you he was going to pay you on Friday. The man always says and does what he says he is going to do, but God you cannot count on. If God says it will come to pass, it may not. We have great confidence in the words of men, and based on their word we will go out telling it all over town.

The power of positive confession works. If you believe that it will come to pass, you have to say it. We receive what we say if we believe it in our hearts. This is the Word of God! That law, Mark 11:23 will work for you whether you are a saint or a sinner because it is a law. As long as you are functioning inside the law, that law is going to work for you. *For assuredly, I say to you, whoever. . .* It did not say whoever Christian, whoever preacher, whoever minister, but rather says, whoever will say. Are you a *whoever*? If you did not know it, I am! I am a *whoever*, so he was talking to me. He said, *whoever* will say, not hope.

"Well, I'm hoping." No, whoever will *say*! "Well, I think. . . ." He did not say think. He said, whoever will *say*.

Yes! Even to the mountain, "*Be removed and be cast into the sea, and does not doubt in his heart, but believes that those things he says will be done, he will have whatever he says.*" Positive or negative, you will have it, if you believe it and say it. I repeat: we need to develop the habit of speaking life instead of death to our lives. Proverbs 6:2 states:

> *You are snared by the words of your mouth;*
> *taken by the words of your mouth.*

You Are Snared by the Words of Your Mouth

Think about it—you are snared or trapped with the words of your mouth. Remember, we have an adversary, Satan, and he is a legalist and will snare you or trap you with your words. Proverbs 6:2 did not say you are snared by the thoughts of your head. It does not become a trap until you say it with your mouth. You could think some thoughts that could ultimately be a trap, if you acted on it. However, it is your mouth that springs that trap!

First Peter 5:8 tells us:

> *Be sober, be vigilant; because your adversary*
> *the devil walks about as a roaring lion, seeking*
> *whom he may devour.*

How will he devour you? He will devour you with the words of your mouth. Satan will keep you bound, poor, sick, and oppressed by the words of your mouth. When you make such negative confessions as "I think I'm gonna be sick.   I hear the Hong

Kong flu is on the way, it'll probably stop at my house." Or, "They have invited us over for dinner and they'll probably have seafood and seafood always makes me sick."

We say things like that, thinking that we are being honest and telling the truth. You don't realize that is how the devil got control of you in the first place in terms of cheating you out of seafood, or whatever. Because you got sick one time, the devil put a thought in your mind that it was the shrimp or the lobster or sea bass is what made you sick. He programmed you through your mind and got you to say it with your mouth.

You should not have any problems eating whatever you want to eat. There may be some things you choose not to eat, but not because it makes you sick.

A true confession of faith
always agrees with the Word of God.

Remember that what you confess or say with your mouth is your faith speaking, and it will reveal whether your faith is weak or strong. You can measure a person by their words. Jesus said one time, and it is true: . . . *For out of the abundance of the heart the mouth speaks* (Matthew 12:34). Whatever is there in abundance will come out through your mouth.

When your confession agrees with the Word of God, then and only then will you receive what God has promised you. A true confession of faith is always based on the Word of the Living God. That is why Satan has so cleverly kept the Word of God out of the churches, because he knows that if people ever find out about the Word of God and begin to believe in their heart that what they say with their mouth will come to pass, then he will be finished lording the negative confessions over them. He will no longer have control over their lives. He will no longer be able to snare them with their words.

God has designed His system to work by His Word. That is why He gave it to us—not to adorn your coffee table; not to be placed on the mantelpiece; not to hold that little red rose that George gave you on your first date. That is not what the Bible is for. God gave us his Word so that we would know His Word, so that we would *believe* His Word, so that we would *say* His Word, so that He could *confirm* His Word in our lives. This is the way the system works. In Mark 16:19-20 the Word of God tells us:

19   *So then, after the Lord had spoken to them* [that is the disciples], *He was received up into heaven, and sat down at the right hand of God.*

20   *And they went out and preached everywhere, the Lord working with them and confirming the word through the accompanying signs. Amen.*

Notice what it does not say. It does not say that He confirmed the people. It said they preached the Word, but God did not confirm them that preached the Word. God confirmed His Word that was preached. It says *accompanying* signs; the Word first, and then the signs.

What most people want is to see some signs first and then they will believe. They say something like, "Well, if I ever see somebody get healed, then I will believe that divine healing is real." However, it doesn't work that way. You have to believe it first, and then you see it. When you see something, why in the world would you have to believe it? "Well, after all, seein' is believin'." No, it is not! Seeing is knowing. Seeing is not believing: seeing is knowing.

"I'll believe it when I see it." Many have said that all their lives. They have heard that from childhood. However, believing has nothing to do with seeing anything. You have to believe it for no other reason than the fact that the Almighty God said it. You have to believe it and then you have to say it, if you want God to get involved in it. That is what makes it work. Therefore, our confession must agree with the Word of God.

A true confession of faith always agrees with the Word of God. Remember this and never forget it; *when my confession agrees with the Word of God, then I will receive what God has promised me.*

Using sickness as an illustration, if you keep hearing all your life that God has put sickness on you to make you a better person, that God put illness on you to help develop you, then you get the idea that God is behind sickness and disease, and He is not. God wants you well, not sick!

How can you agree with God when you do not know what He says? As a result of ignorance, you go around saying, "Well, the Lord put this on me. I know God is testing me." The truth is that God is not involved in it. He cannot confirm sickness or disease because it is not His Word. What has really happened is that you are trapped by the words of your mouth, snared by your words. You are speaking death to your life instead of life—and you do not even know it!

CHAPTER THREE

GOD CANNOT LIE!

S ince the original Greek word for the word *confession* as it is used in the New Testament means "to agree with," or "say the same thing that God says," I will be continually referring to this fact throughout this book.

The Bible says it is impossible for God to lie. If it is impossible for God to lie, the only alternative is that God must tell the truth. If God says something about me, then that must be who I am, what I have, and what I can do. If God says I can do it, I can do it. If God says I have it, I have it.

If God says that is who I am, then that is who I am.

At the time that I find out what God says about me or the situation, I might not be experiencing any of it in my personal life. However, that is irrelevant and immaterial. What the Word of God says about me is still who I am because God sees the end from the beginning, and the beginning from the end. And, since God cannot lie, but only tell the truth, then what He says about me must be who I am.

If I will have the spiritual sense to bring my mouth, my confession—the words that I say in line with what God says I am, I have, and I can do—the things that I find in His Word—I will have that manifested in my personal everyday life. That is exactly the way it works. That is a divine law. We need to form the habit and we need to stay with it—of agreeing with what God says.

I do not know about you, but I have been down and now I am up, and up is better! I have been sick and now I am well, and well is better. Learning about confession has so dramatically changed my life—the difference between what I was before I found out about confession and what I have become since I found out about it is so dramatic. It is almost as dramatic as the change between when I was a sinner and when I accepted Christ and received salvation. I have personally experienced what I am talking about in regard to confession. I am not giving you theory, or "I think," "It could be," "Maybe so if all other conditions are met." I am telling you what I know to be true.

Even though I began to operate in this law of confession, it sounded strange to me when I first heard it. How could what I say have anything to do with what I have and what I experience in my life? However, God said it, so I began to say it. I said, "I don't have anything to lose, I'm already down for the count. The enemy's standing on my chest with his boot on my neck." I had absolutely nothing to lose.

More than 30 years ago, I began saying what God said, and I am telling you the truth, it was miraculous, the change that took place in my own personal life. As a result, I am committed to the proposition that this is one of the most important truths that God has revealed to us in His Word, and yet, it is so misunderstood.

NAME IT AND CLAIM IT—OR YOU GET NOTHING!

Every once in a while, there are some who make fun of, poke fun at, and criticize this law of confession. A minister was heard to say this about yours truly, Fred Price: "That's the 'name it and claim it' bunch!" Hey! If that is who I am, I accept the name because it is true. It is name it and claim it.

I do not deal with the criticizers because of the criticism, but to show you how people can miss God. To illustrate: when you go to the Will Call, you had better name and claim what is yours, or you will not get anything. "I bought a bicycle. It's red. It's an ABC bicycle made on Mars. Here's my receipt, I want it!" I named and claimed it and that is what they gave me. They did not bring me an elephant, or a hippopotamus, or a rhinoceros, or a speed boat. They brought me a bicycle, a red bicycle because that is the one I bought and my receipt shows that I paid for it. I named it, I claimed it, and I got it!

If I had walked up to the Will Call window and said, "Hey, I want to pick up my merchandise," they would have asked, "What's your name?" "I have no name." "Well, what's the merchandise?" "I don't know."

If this scenario had taken place, what would I have received? Nothing. In an example like this, we have no problem understanding. We can understand because we are so intelligent, so erudite and scholarly. However, when it comes to the things of God, suddenly it is a dilemma for us.

Name it and claim it? You better believe it! I am the name-it-and- claim-it man! Everything I have truly desired over the last 30 years, I have named it, claimed it, and I got it. But, maybe it just works for me. Maybe I am God's special child.

Your Uncle Rufus, a multimillionaire, whom you have not seen in 25 years, died and left you 10 million dollars. You had better go name it and claim it or you will not get it! You had better go wherever the will is being read and let those folk know, "Hey, I'm the one Uncle Rufus was talking about. Here's my I.D. I claim my inheritance."

In the same manner you can name and claim what God said you can name and claim. You do not just arbitrarily go off and name and claim any old thing. When you park your car, the attendant gives you a claim check. When you come back, you cannot say, "I want that Rolls-Royce sitting over there," Do you think they are going to give you the Rolls-Royce? No way! They will only give you the car you have a claim check for. You have a claim check that matches the one that is stuck under your windshield wiper blade. The numbers had better match up or the attendant is a fool if he gives you someone else's car.

. . . there is a negative end to laws as well as a positive end.

Remember, all laws have a reciprocal. They all work in reverse. Did you know that? In other words, there is a negative end to laws as well as a positive end. Many people do not realize that, but everything they have in life is because of what they have named and claimed over the years.

You must realize that laws work whether you know they are working or not. Laws are not laws and valid because you know them. They work whether you know they are working or not.

In our society, we have been programmed—without realizing it—to name it and claim it. People told us something about ourselves and we named it and claimed it: "I'll never amount to anything because none of the males in our family have ever amounted to anything. They have all been failures, so I'll probably be a failure." "Granddaddy was a wino, my daddy was an alcoholic and I'll probably be one too."

You named that and claimed that. "We have never had anything in our family, we've always been poor. I'm a third-generation welfare recipient. My kids will probably be fourth-generation welfare recipients." Again, they named it and claimed it. They did not know that was what they were doing, but a rose by any other name is still a rose.

First John 1:9 says:

> *If we confess our sins, He is faithful and*
> *just to forgive us our sins and to*
> *cleanse us from all unrighteousness.*

God is the One Who wrote the Bible. *He said, If we confess our sins, He is faithful and just to forgive us.* That means that when I sin, I have to say I sinned and ask God for forgiveness. It is not until I say I have sinned that I get the forgiveness.

God says certain things are sin. For instance, fornication is sin. God said it in His Word. If I commit fornication, when I say that it is a sin and ask God for forgiveness, then I am agreeing with God, and only then will I be forgiven. If God says that stealing is a sin, you have to say, "Stealing is a sin." If you steal, then you have to say, "I have sinned and ask God for forgiveness" and it is not until then that you will receive forgiveness.

Psalm 103:1-3 say:

> 1   *Bless the LORD, O my soul; and all*
> *that is within me, bless His holy name!*

2   *Bless the LORD, O my soul, and forget*
       not all His benefits:

3   *Who forgives all your iniquities, Who*
       heals all your diseases,

From the scripture, it is obvious there is a discrepancy between the traditionally held idea that God is the One Who makes us sick for some divine purpose. If God is the One Who makes us sick as well as the One Who heals all our diseases, we have a problem. Healing cancels out disease and sickness, and whatever benefit God has in mind for making us sick is lost! Psalm 103:1-3 clearly shows that God is not in the business of making us sick. God is the healer, not the afflicter—even though He has been accused of it traditionally.

Notice what the third verse says: *Who forgives all your iniquities, Who heals all your diseases.* When a sickness or a disease attacks my body, even though the circumstances may say I am sick, I have to say what God says about the condition if I am going to be released from it. If I say, "I am sick," then I am saying that sickness is mine. What I have to do is say what God says. "I believe I am healed of this condition. I believe I am well in Jesus' name."

This is what we must say if we are going to get that healing, physically manifested in our lives. In James 5:14-15 the Word of God says, *Is anyone among you sick? Let him call for the elders of the church, and let them pray over him, anointing him with oil in the name of the Lord. And the prayer of faith will save the sick, and the Lord will raise him up. And if he has committed sins, he will be forgiven.*

Understand this; you do not have to anoint people with oil. That is just one of the many methods God has placed in the Body of Christ because He wants us healed. People are at varying levels of spiritual understanding, and while one method would work on one level, it would not work on another level.

God has made enough methods available so that wherever you are in terms of your knowledge and spiritual development, there is a method that can reach you. The highest method, of course, is to believe God for yourself. God says He will raise me up. I have to say that, and then act according to His Word.

First Peter 2:24:
> who Himself bore our sins in His own body on
> the tree, that we, having died to sins, might live
> for righteousness; by whose stripes you were healed.

If you know anything about elementary English, you know that the word *were* is a past-tense term, and is indicative of the fact that the time of action has already taken place. It is not taking place, it is not going to take place, it is already an accomplished fact. "We are healed."

As I said before, God cannot lie. Therefore, the only alternative is that God tells the truth. If God says I am healed with Jesus' stripes, then either I am healed or God is a liar. If I was, I am. And, if I am, I "is" healed. That is not proper English, but with the word "is" you know that we are talking about *now*.

In all the churches that I matriculated through over a 17-year period, I was never told that I was supposed to say what God said about me. I thought I was supposed to say what the circumstances said about me, what the doctors said about me, what the newspapers said about me, what the history books said about me, what the white folks said about me, what the black folks said about me. I thought I was supposed to say what my mama, my friends, and my enemies said about me.

I did not know I was supposed to say what my heavenly Father said about me, so I never said what He said about me. When the circumstances came in like a flood and said I was sick, I would say, "I'm sick!" "How do you feel?" "I'm sick!" "You don't look too well." "I'm sick!" "Are you going to work today?" "I'm sick!"

I confessed that because I was a truthful person. I wanted to tell the truth. I did not want to deliberately lie. The circumstances told me I was sick because I was hurting. However, all the time that was going on in my body, God's Word never changed. It said the same thing: *by whose stripes you were healed.* This lets me know that I am healed *now.* Did you notice what this verse does not say? It does not say "by whose stripes you were healed if you look or feel like you are healed. " It says *by whose stripes you were healed.*

Therefore, I started saying what God said. I figured I had nothing to lose. If confession does not work, I am going to be sick anyway, so I might as well say what God's says. I began to say, "I believe I am healed." And, do you know circumstances began to change! Do you know that in the 30 years that I have been pastor of Crenshaw Christian Center, I have never missed a Sunday morning service ministering the Word—other than when I was either on vacation, ministering at the New York church or out of the country. Other than that, I have never missed being at my job on Sunday mornings. I have never missed my Tuesday night Bible class because of any physical condition because I believe I am well.

I never said I was not attacked. I never said that there are not times that I am experiencing pain. There have been many times when I have been ministering and felt like 17-miles of unpaved road. Every step I took and every word I spoke was painful. I had to agree in my heart—my spirit—with what God says and I have noticed that when I do this that the anointing power of God puts me over. It I were to ever stop and wait until I feel perfectly well before I initiate any activity, I would never feel well. Satan would have me right where he wants me under his feet. Instead, I have to act like I am well.

I ask myself, "What would I do if I were actually well, with no pain in my body, nothing hindering me physically?" I would be doing my job. I would be going on vacation, making love to my wife, hugging my kids, playing with the frog if I had a frog, petting the dog if I had a dog, and stroking the cat if I had a cat. I would be doing what I normally do, right?

God said that with His stripes I was healed. I believe what God said, so I cannot be in bed in traction. I have to get up and go and do, and I have done it.

I have crawled out of the bed when I felt like I was going to die. In fact, I felt like dying would be better. Dying would have been painless compared to what I was experiencing at the time. In spite of it, I said, "I believe I am well, so I have to get up and go." And, while I am going is when suddenly I realize, "Hey! You know, I don't hurt anymore. Where did the pain go?"

God said it, I must say it and that is when I get it. In Mark 11:24, Jesus says, "*Therefore I say to you, whatever things you ask when you pray, believe that you receive them, and you will have them.*" This is a positive and God said that I could have what I ask for. If you look at the scriptures in total concerning asking, the qualifying statement would be this—and I am paraphrasing it—"I can have what I ask for as long as what I ask for is consistent with a godly life."

GOD'S WORD OUGHT TO PRODUCE RESULTS

There are two ways to understand the ways of God. One is by reading and believing His Word. The second is to experience God's Word.

There should be a time, somewhere in my life, when I actually experience what God says in His Word. If His Word is true, if it is valid and if I do what He says, it has to produce a tangible result in my life, somewhere, sometime. If 100 years pass and I keep believing and confessing God's Word and never receive anything that God's Word says I should receive, then there could be some serious doubts as to whether or not it is really true.

By operating in the power of positive confession and observing God's Word, I have received everything that I have ever personally desired. I have always made sure that my desires were consistent with a godly life. And, I always made sure that what I desired I could find a basis for in the Word of God.

Philippians 4:19 says, *and my God shall supply all your need. . . .* And there is a way you can put your needs and desires together. You cannot find in the Bible where it specifically says that God will give you a Bentley, Cadillac, Mercedes-Benz, Maserati, Rolls-Royce, or a Volkswagen. However, it does say He will supply your *need.*

I have a need for a vehicle so that I can be independent of public transportation and be able to go to work and come home when I want to. I could believe God for an automobile because that is a need. He said He would supply all of my need for transportation. He also said *whatsoever things I desire.*

Since I have a need for "wheels," why not go ahead and desire the best wheels that are rolling? Beauty is in the eye of the beholder. The Rolls-Royce was the best in my opinion at that time. So, I believed God for a Rolls-Royce and He gave me one and I did not have to pay a dime for it. He gave it to me because I asked Him for it. Then recently, I was blessed with a Bentley for my 70th birthday. Confession works when you are doing God's Word.

YOUR FAITH WILL NEVER RISE ABOVE
THE LEVEL OF YOUR CONFESSION

There is a spiritual law that says, "Your faith will never rise above the level of your confession." As you read this statement again, say it out loud and make it personal: "My faith will never rise above the level of my confession."

Again, looking at Mark 11:24, Jesus said, *"Therefore I say to you, whatever things you ask when you pray, believe that you receive them, and you will have them."* Right away someone will challenge you by saying it is dishonest to say that they believe they are healed when they have pain in their body. Mentally, some people have a real problem with this concept. The reason they have a problem is that they miss one very small, but important item about Mark 11:24.

Jesus said that if you believe that you receive them, you will have them. It is obvious that you do not have it when you pray about it, because if you actually physically had it when you prayed, then you would not have to "will have" it later. Understand that "will have" is a future- tense designation, indicating that the time of action has not yet taken place, but will take place in the future.

He did not say when you pray *feel* like you are well. He said, *believe* it. Again, the point I am making is if He had said "feel like it," and you still had pain, then you would be telling a lie. He did not even say when you pray, *know* it. He did not say when you pray *see* it. He did not say when you pray, *understand* it. He said *believe* it! Believe you receive it, and then you will have it.

It you do not have it already, you cannot say you have it. You have to say, "I believe I have it." "I believe I have it" is a confession of faith. It is not a confession of physical fact. Therefore, when I am attacked with sickness, I go to the Word of God, and God says in I Peter 2:24, . . .*by whose stripes you were healed.* Then I have to speak life to my life, according to Proverbs 18:21: *Death and life are in the power of the tongue.*

I have to believe that what God says about me is true because the Bible says that it is impossible for God to lie. Therefore, if it is impossible for God to lie, the only alternative is that God must tell the truth. As a result, I must be healed whether I look like it, or whether I feel like it, or whether I see it, or whether I understand it or not. If I am not healed, then God is a liar.

You might think it does not make sense, but thank God a thousand times over the fact that it does not have to make sense. Because if it had to make sense we would all be up the creek in a boat with no oars.

I am not telling a lie when I say I believe I am healed. I only talk about what I believe, and what I believe is based on what God says in His Word. In the natural sense, we do this every day and never question it. We normally give other people the benefit of the doubt and act on what they say on our behalf, and give them the chance to make it good. However, when it comes to God, we want God to prove it to us first, and then we will accept it.

When you go to the airport and buy a ticket to go somewhere, you do not tell the airline to "prove to me you are going to take me to New York City." You will never know until you get on the plane and arrive in New York City. You have to take them at their word. You have to act on their word.

When you begin working for a company and they say they will pay you $500 per week, they usually do not pay you the money before you do the work. I guarantee you, you did not spend any time fasting and praying that first week leading up to payday praying about whether or not the company will have enough money in the bank to pay you at the end of the week. In fact, to show you how much confidence you have in the word of those people, whom you did not even know, you go out and begin telling your friends, "See me next week, I'm going to get paid on Friday." Now that is amazing!

We know for a fact, between Monday and Friday, many companies have failed and gone into bankruptcy, filing Chapters 7, 8, 9 and 11; they had no money in the bank to pay their employees. Yet, you cannot find one time where God ever failed to honor His Word.

There are passages in the Bible which tell us that we have an adversary who is Satan. He is called the god of this world. This world that we live in is a three-dimensional, physical, tangible, material world. Satan is the god who operates through the material world and he operates through the material world to get to us. Without realizing it, when you confess or speak the negative circumstances, you are opening the door and giving Satan a license to fulfill what you are saying with your mouth.

Do not misunderstand me, though, because if I am actually sick, I am sick! It I were not actually sick, I would not need to be healed. Correct? And, God is acknowledging that there is sickness and disease because He said, with Jesus' stripes you were healed. How could you be healed of something that does not exist? The very fact that you were healed with Jesus' stripes indicates the reality of sickness and disease. Do you understand that?

When God said with Jesus' stripes you were healed; when He said, lay hands on the sick and they will recover, lets us know that there are people that need recovering from something.

WHAT MAKES GOD'S POWER WORK?

What makes God's power work is not for us to talk or confess the negative circumstances (what we see, what we feel, and what we are experiencing), but rather, confess God's remedy, God's cure for the situation. This is what changes the situation, and that is what faith is all about.

When I say what God says, I am not telling a lie. If I have pain and I say I do not have pain, I am lying. I am a liar. However, if I say, "I believe I am healed," even though I have a temperature of 105, even though I hurt, I am not telling a lie, because I am not talking about how I feel. If I said I did not hurt when, in fact, I did hurt, I would be telling a lie.

If I prayed three days ago according to Mark 11:24 and I believed that I received my healing I must now make my confession of faith, "I believe that I am healed."

Remember that Hebrews 11:1 says; *Now faith is. . . .* Therefore, I have to keep confession in the present tense. At that point I will be speaking life to my life. I will be a making a positive confession based on God's Word.

WHAT IF PEOPLE THINK YOU ARE STRANGE?

It takes time to program yourself to confess God's Word instead of the circumstances, but the rewards and the benefits are astounding. You have nothing to lose but your negative situation.

If what I have been talking about did not work, and you said, "I believe I'm healed" when you were sick, you would not be any worse off, because you are still sick and still hurting. Therefore, you might as well say it: "Praise God, I believe I'm healed!"

As I told you before, 30 years ago, I began finding out what God said about me, and I began confessing what He said about me. Since God cannot lie, I began to say, "That's me! Praise God, I'm blessed going out and blessed coming in. I'm the head and not the tail. I'm blessed in the city and blessed in the field. I believe I'm healed from the top of my head to the soles of my feet. I believe God shall supply all my need according to His riches in glory by Christ Jesus."

The reason you have to say it is because there is a divine law in Romans 10:17 that says, *So then faith comes by hearing, and hearing by the word of God.* I do not know about you, but I have more confidence in my word than I do in anyone else's. I know my word is good. I absolutely, positively know it.

What is the point I am making? The point is that if I say "I believe I'm healed," don't you know I just heard myself say that? And, if I have confidence in anyone's word, I ought to have confidence in mine. Every time I say it, I hear it and every time I hear it, it is reinforcing my faith on that subject, so I have to say it out loud to get the faith benefit.

Right away, someone might say, "But what are people gonna think if they hear me say that?" Well, that is the bottom line, you have to make a decision as to who you are going to please — people or God? Yes, people will think you are strange, but they will think you are strange while you are filing for bankruptcy, so they might as well think you are strange for doing something that is going to benefit you. Besides that, you cannot control what people think.

No matter what you do, everyone will not always think you are right. Someone will think you are a crook anyway. If you worry about what people think, you will be in trouble for sure. You have to think about you and the Lord. You have to begin to say what God says about you.

Remember: Your faith will never rise above the level of your confession.

CHAPTER FOUR

AND GOD SAID . . .

I know I quote Mark 11:24 a lot and refer to it often, but that is because it is such an important principle for the Body of Christ to follow. However, I want you to see that this biblical principle is enunciated in other scriptures as well.

First John 5:14-15:

14   *Now this is the confidence that we have*

    in Him, that if we ask anything according

    to His will [doesn't *ask anything* sound something

like *whatsoever things*?] *He hears us.*

15   *And it we know that He hears us, whatever*
[whatever sounds like anything, sounds
like whatsoever] we ask, we know that we have
the petitions that we have asked of Him.

Notice what it does not say. It does not say we know that we are going to get it. It says, we know that we have! You might say, "But I don't see it." That is why you have faith because, according to Hebrews 11:1, faith is the evidence of things not seen.

"But I can't believe that I have something that I can't see." Have you ever seen your brain? You say you have brains. . . . Prove it! Let us see it. Let me see your brain. How do you know you have a brain? You have been told that all your life, but you were told a lot of other things all your life and found out later that they were not true. Like the fat cat in the red suit coming down the chimney, flying through the sky with reindeers to bring you Christmas gifts. How do you know you have a brain? Maybe they have been lying to us all the time. Do you have lungs? Have you ever seen your lungs? How do you know that you have a pituitary gland? Do you have veins and arteries in your body? How do you know? Have you seen them? Have you ever seen your spinal cord? No! Somebody told you that you have one and you believe it.

Verse 15 again, *And if we know.* . . . What does *know* mean? It means a foregone conclusion. It is absolute. There is no debate, no argument. First John 5:15 says, *And if we know that He hears us, whatever we ask, we know that we have the petitions that we have asked of Him.* If God says I have it, then I have it. I cannot stress this point enough. If God says I have it, then, I have it!

What I have to do is begin to speak life to my life. Begin to speak what God says. When we pray, He tells us to . . . *ask anything according to His will* . . . Anything! That would include healing, my financial needs met and family relationship needs met; it would include everything. I have to believe I have it because He said I do.

And if we know that He hears us, whatever
we ask, we know that wehave the petitions . . . .

We have it. How? We have it by faith.

GOD WANTS US TO COPY HIM

By faith we say, "Praise God, I believe my need is met." "Praise God, I believe I am healed." Praise God, I believe, I believe, I believe. . . whatever it is. You have to begin to say that, and begin to see yourself with it. Begin to take God at His Word, and when you do that, you will be the recipient of the thing your heart desires.

Why is it that God wants us to say things with our mouths? He wants us to pattern ourselves after Him because everything He ever did, He did it with His mouth. He did it by His words.

Go back and read the first chapter of Genesis. Throughout that chapter, you will continually read where it says, and *God said, and God said, and God said.* If you are very astute and observant about your reading, you will notice that nothing came into being in that chapter until after God said it. This is very interesting.

Natural human rationale would say, "All right, God is God, He is a super Being. He has supernatural abilities. All He has to do is wave His hand and things will come to pass. Snap His fingers, and boom, there would be the dry land. Zap! There would be the stars." However, it is interesting that the Bible records that God prefaced all of His creation by words. *Then God said, "Let there be light"; and there was light,* but light did not appear until after God said it.

Why did He record this in the Bible? Because He wants the children to act like the parents. You know that is what children do. Children act like their parents, especially if they have a relatively good home situation where the father and mother are both in the home. Children will emulate their parents. Parents are really the child's first example of God that he or she has.

God wants us to copy Him. God is a talker. God is a "sayer."

God said, Let there be .... Be what? "Let there be divine health in my body. *Let there be* .... Be what? "Let there be no sickness or disease in my body." However, I need to *say* it!

Remember, God requires us to confess not what we feel, not what we see, not what we understand, but what His Word says because our faith will never rise above the level of our confession.

Satan is a squatter. . . . He will set up housekeeping right in the empty void in your life.

Think about it, if you are not saying anything, you will not get anything. When you do not say it (what God says), then you create a void and that is when Satan moves in. Satan is a squatter who will move right in and take over. He will set up housekeeping right in that empty void of your life. This is why you must say it and have to say it all the time.

It has to become a habit with you. You have to train yourself, discipline yourself to say it. In the natural sense, sometimes I get tired of saying, "I believe I am healed," but I do not get tired of being healed, so I keep saying it. I got tired of being sick, so I found out that if I say I am healed, my faith confession promotes the manifestation of my heart's desire. Please note, my confession of what God says in His Word is my faith speaking, and that is what causes it to come to pass or be physically manifested in my life. My confessions are what make it work. You have to be a talker. Some people say, "I don't like to talk." Then go without!

In all situations, we must always remember that our confession must be based on what God says in His Word. You may say, "Does that mean that I cannot have any thoughts of my own, that God doesn't want me to think on my own?" No! It could not mean that, because that is why He gave you that head full of sand—otherwise, called a brain. He wants you to think. However, bring your thinking into line with God's thinking. You still put it into your own words, but it will be God's principles. What is wrong with that? Nothing, because you do that all the time anyway.

You do the things you see in the movies, on television, things you hear in songs. Many of the words and phrases that you use, you picked up by listening to the radio, TV, on the Internet or wherever. You heard something that sounded good and you began adopting that into your own life. This is all right, as long as it is a positive statement.

Some people want to be original about everything. I do not care about being original. If I come up with something original, that is all well and good, but if I do not, I am not going to go without. I will use yours if it is not nailed down! I do not have a problem with it. However, some people, if they did not invent it or think of it first, then it is no good.

Another biblical example is found in Exodus 15:26, where it states:

> *"If you diligently heed the voice of the LORD*
> *your God and do what is right in His sight,*
> *give ear to His commandments and keep all His*
> *statutes, I will put none of the diseases on you*
> *which I have brought on the Egyptians. For I am*
> *the LORD who heals you."*

Unfortunately, when this was translated from the original Hebrew into English, every word was not always translated to its fullest extent. Why? I do not know.

However, Dr. Robert Young, a Hebrew and Greek scholar, who also wrote *Young's Concordance,* tells us that Exodus 15:26 (and many other verses) have been translated in the "causative sense" instead of the "permissive sense" as they should have been. It is obvious from the Bible, and even human history, that God does not cause sickness and disease, but He does permit it.

Exodus 15:26 should have been translated thusly:

> *"If you diligently heed the voice of the LORD*
> *your God and do what is right in His sight, give*
> *ear to His commandments and keep all His*
> *statutes, I will put* [permit] *none of the*
> *diseases on you which I have brought*
> [permitted] *on the Egyptians. For* [Because]
> *I am the LORD who heals you."*

If God is the Lord who heals you, He cannot at the same time be the Lord Who makes you sick. He would be working at cross purposes with Himself. Not only that, but the Bible tells us in James 1:17 that:

> *Every good gift and every perfect gift is*
> *from above, and comes down from the Father*
> *of lights, with whom there is no variation or*
> *shadow of turning.*

Since every good and perfect gift comes down from God, sickness could not come from above, because there is nothing good or perfect about sickness and disease, and I certainly would not call it a gift. Would you? As another example of what we can and should confess is found in Psalm 103:2-3:

> 2   *Bless the LORD, O my soul, and forget not all*
>   *His benefits:*

> 3   *Who forgives all your iniquities, Who heals*
>   *all your diseases,*

What I have learned to do when reading the Bible where it says, "your." I put my name in there. In other words: Who heals all Fred's diseases. He is talking to me. This is for me. This is for Fred. So I say, "Praise God, thank You, Father, for healing all my diseases. Who forgives all Fred's iniquities, who heals all Fred's diseases." I have to believe this, and I have to confess it, if I ever expect to have it manifested in my daily life.

Isaiah 53:1-5 says:

1   *Who has believed our report? And to whom has the arm of the LORD been revealed?*

2   *For He shall grow up before Him as a tender plant, and as a root out of dry ground. He has no form or comeliness; and when we see Him, there is no beauty that we should desire Him.*

3   *He is despised and rejected by men, a Man of sorrows and acquainted with grief. And we hid, as it were, our faces from Him; He was despised, and we did not esteem Him.*

4   *Surely He has borne our griefs and carried our sorrows; yet we esteemed Him stricken, smitten by God, and afflicted.*

5   *But He was wounded for our transgressions, He was bruised for our iniquities; the chastisement for our peace was upon Him, and by His stripes we are healed.*

You have to see that personally. Notice verse 5: *But He was wounded for **our transgressions**, He was bruised for **our iniquities**; the chastisement for our peace was **upon Him**, and **by His stripes** we are healed.* Do you realize that in every one of those four designations, it is clear that the reason why Jesus took those things is so that we would not have to? God is not a masochist. He does not want both His Only Begotten Son and us to pay for the same crime twice! Even in the natural world, people do not believe in paying for the same thing twice.

It says that Jesus was wounded for our transgressions. Not for His—but for ours! Why would He be wounded for ours? So that we would not have to be wounded. He was bruised for our iniquities. He did it on our behalf. The chastisement of our peace was upon Him so that we would not have to be chastised, and with His stripes, we are healed.

If we are healed, then we are not sick. Because we cannot be healed and sick at the same time. You are either one or the other, not both. The reason you need to be healed is because you are sick. However, if you are sick and get healed, the reason you get healed is so that you won't be sick anymore. If you have healing, you do not have sickness. If you have sickness, you do not have healing. You have one or the other, not both. You either have light or dark. You cannot have both of them at the same point in time and space. It is impossible.

In the Gospel of Matthew, we have the fulfillment of Isaiah 53.

Matthew 8:16-17 tell us:

16   *When evening had come, they brought to Him many who were demon-possessed. And He cast out the spirits with a word, and healed all who were sick,*

17   *that it might be fulfilled which was spoken by Isaiah the prophet, saying: "He Himself took our infirmities and bore our sicknesses."*

Based upon that, my confession is, "Praise God, thank You, Father that Jesus Himself took my infirmities and bore my sicknesses."

Notice here it says, *Himself took* . . . the word *took* is a past-tense designation. If it had said Himself *will take,* that would be future tense. If it said, Himself *is* taking, that would be present tense, but it says, *Himself took.* . . . That is past tense, and in the mind of God He has already done it! As a result, I say, again, "Praise God! Father, I thank You that Jesus took all my infirmities." If He took them all, I do not have any. Therefore, I confess I am free and that I have no infirmities.

Do Not Accept Sickness or Disease!

Satan has no legal right to put sickness and infirmities on us. We do not have to accept sickness and disease. I realize that this is a "bomb" and some people cannot handle it. People get upset when you say that you do not have to be sick. If you are going to worry about what people say, go ahead and be sick. We do not need to argue about the matter. You can be sick if you want to. Every Christian has to make a choice to be sick or walk in healing.

You can be just as sick as you want to be. In fact, you can get so sick you can die from it. It is *your* choice. However, do not begrudge me. If I want to delude myself and deceive myself into thinking I can be well, so what? I am giving God all the glory. You are sick and dying and giving God the glory. I believe I am well, and I am supposed to be well, and I will always be well, and I am giving God the glory. So, what is the problem?

Here is another healing illustration found in James 5:14-15:

14   *Is anyone among you sick? Let him call for the elders of the church, and let them pray over him* [for what?], *anointing him with oil in the name of the Lord* [for what?].

15   *And the prayer of faith will save the sick,*
       and the Lord will raise him up. And if he
       has committed sins, he will be forgiven.

Anyone sick refers to anybody—male, female, man, woman, boy, girl, black, white, brown, red, yellow, old, young, rich, poor, educated, uneducated, apartment dweller, single-family residence dweller, camper dweller, trailer court dweller—anybody! Let him call for the elders of the church and let them pray over him, anointing him with oil in the name of the Lord: and the prayer of faith will save the sick. That is the key—the prayer of faith!

You do not have to anoint with oil, but you can. It is just one of the many ways God has made available for us to be healed. God wants us well to such an extent that He has not limited Himself to just one channel by which He can bring healing to us, but He has a variety of ways. No matter where your faith is, there is a way to reach you. This is what is exciting to me.

What is the oil for? The oil acts as a point of contact through which God can move. See, some of us are so earthly bound and so physically oriented that it takes something tangible for us to release our faith, so God accommodates us. He comes down to our level of faith. The oil is not anointed; the oil is not what is important. What is important is our *faith*.

It is the prayer of faith that heals the sick. It did not say the oil would. Faith heals, not the oil. Thank God, the prayer of faith will heal the sick, so I have to believe that and *say* it, if it is to work for me. First Peter 2:24 is a very familiar scripture, but again, it is just an example of the kind of things that we need to learn how to speak into our lives.

> *who Himself bore our sins in His own body on the*
> *tree, that we, having died to sins, might live for*
> *righteousness; by whose stripes you were healed.*

If this is not God's will, what is it? I have heard some say, "That scripture is not talking about physical healing, Brother Price. It is talking about spiritual healing." That sounds plausible, but it is not tenable relative to the Word of God, because nowhere in the Bible, from Genesis to Revelation, does it ever tell us or even suggest that God heals sick spirits.

When Jesus walked this earth, He said, He who has seen Me has seen the Father (John 14:9). No, He did not mean that the Father looked like Jesus physically, but what He meant was that when you see Him in action and hear His Words, you are seeing the Father. He said, I have come down from heaven, not to do My own will, but the will of Him who sent Me (John 6:38). In fact, He went so far as to say, it is not even me doing the works, the Father who dwells in Me does the works (John 14:10).

If healing were for the spirit of man and not for the physical body of man, then somewhere along the line, it seems like God would have helped us out by giving us at least one example of it. You do not find one place anywhere in the four Gospels where Jesus, or His disciples, healed anybody spiritually. Leprosy is not a spiritual sickness; it manifests itself in the human flesh. Deafness is not something that is in the spirit. It is physical bodies that go deaf. It is not lame spirits, but it is lame physical bodies that need restoring.

In reference to 1 Peter 2:24 again, *who Himself bore our sins in His own body . . . .* Understand that sin has to do with the spirit and spiritual relationship with God. That is understandable and that is understood by the Word of God. However, what is God saying? The results of sin are manifested in the physical body.

At the pool of Bethesda, Jesus found the man who had a condition for 38 years. Jesus said to the man, *"Do you want to be made well?"* and the man answered, *"Sir, I have no man to put me into the pool when the water is stirred up . . . ."* And Jesus looked at him and said, *"Rise, take up your bed and walk"* (John 5:6-8). And, the man was instantly healed and went his way. Jesus conveyed Himself away, according to the scripture, into the crowd. Later on, Jesus met up with the man again. What did Jesus say to the man? *He said, "Sin no more, lest a worse thing come upon you"* (John 5:14).

What was wrong with the man? He was lame and could not walk. He was a paralytic. Jesus said, "Do not sin anymore lest something worse come upon you." Worse what? Worse physically. You could be deaf, dumb, blind, aa well as lame. That would be worse than just being lame.

With Jesus' stripes you were healed. *Were* is past tense, and if you *were*, you *are*, and if you *are*, you *is*. I know this is not proper English, but it helps me to understand it more clearly. What this scripture is saying is that I am healed right now. Therefore, I say, "I believe that I am healed." I am speaking life to my life.

When sickness and disease try to assault my body, I stand toe to toe and eyeball to eyeball, and nose to nose with it, and I say to the sickness and disease monster that comes against me: "You foul spirit of infirmity, you are defeated. You are whipped. I am healed in the name of Jesus. Get away from me. You are trespassing on holy ground." You have to say it if you want God's

power to work for you! Yes, but that sounds strange. I do not care how it sounds. I am not interested in how it sounds. I am interested in results.

"But people might think I'm not very smart saying that." Who cares what people think? I am only concerned about what God thinks. That is all we need to be concerned about. This is where our help is coming from. Help is not coming from folk. All you will get from people is criticism, misunderstanding, false accusations, jealousy, pride, envy and strife. And, none of these will help you.

Some people are having a problem understanding this principle and they say, "But I don't understand how I can maintain a positive confession of healing when I don't feel healed. I don't understand. Wouldn't I be telling a lie? Wouldn't I be lying about it if I said I believe I am healed and my temperature is 105 and I'm aching all over?"

Many Christians have a problem saying, "I believe I am healed," based on the Word of God. Yet a person can go into the hospital having been diagnosed with some debilitating problem in

AND GOD SAID ...

his body. They can be remanded over to surgery because the doctor has told them that there is a malignant tumor. The doctor tells you, "We believe that based upon its size and location that we can successfully remove it in its entirety and that you can— all other things being equal—continue to lead a normal and fulfilling life."

TRUSTING THE DOCTOR'S WORD OVER JESUS' WORD

Based upon what the doctors say, the person goes into the hospital for surgery. The doctor performs a five-and-one-half-hour operation on the individual. The doctor cuts him open, reaches into his abdominal cavity and removes the tumor, sews him up and sends him to the recovery room. He goes through the recovery and is finally placed in a ward. He is under intensive care for a while because he was in such bad shape. His body has to have time to recover.

The person is watched and his vital signs are monitored. The doctor comes in, examines him and a few days later, he is in a private room. His friends, relatives, wife and children come to see him while he is lying in bed. The patient does not look too good. He looks like somebody who has gone through a traumatic experience, and he has. It has been a shock to his system to be cut open like that. When the friends come into the room, they ask, "Well, how are you doing?" And the patient answers, "Oh, I'm doing just fine. The doctor got the whole tumor out. The doctor said I'll be going home in about three weeks."

Now, is this patient lying? Yes, he is! He is lying because he is in pain. He is using pain pills every half hour. There is soreness where that incision was made, where those tubes have been injected into the body. The person does not feel well. He does not look good. He does not feel like everything is all right, but yet he is saying, "I'm all right; the doctors got it all out." Why? Because the doctor said so. The doctor said they got the whole tumor out.

You did not see the tumor being taken out. You did not see, with your own eyes, the operation being performed. You were

61

under anesthesia. You do not know what they took out. They may have put something in instead of taking something out. However, you are taking the word of the doctor—a mere man!

You have trusted your life into the hands of this man who is supposed to be a medical professional, and he says you are all right. "We got it all out. There is no more malignancy in your body." Nevertheless, you are still in pain. You are still hurting. You are still physically off balance. Your head is rocking and reeling from the medication and anesthesia. However, you are telling everybody, "I'm all right. I'm going back to work in about 30 days. I'll be home in about three weeks." Why? Because the doctor said so.

Well, God has told you that you are healed through Dr. Jesus! Why are you having such a problem saying what He says: "I believe I'm healed? With Jesus stripes I was healed."

If it is okay for you to say that you are all right because the doctor said so, yet you are still in pain, your body is not well yet, but you are confessing what the doctor said. Are you lying? You are basing your confession on the word of someone you have respect for. Someone you feel knows what they are talking about, a medically trained professional.

Likewise, what is wrong with me saying, "I believe I'm healed?" I have the test result from the laboratory. It said, with Jesus' stripes I was healed. Yes, I have pain in my body. Yes, I still have the incision where the operation was performed, but the Master got it all out! I believe I am well. Why am I lying when I say what God says, but telling the truth when I say what the doctor says? We trust the word of man and make confessions based upon what they tell us. Why will we not trust the Word of the Chief Resident Surgeon of all the ages? Hallelujah! I rest my case.

A negative confession nullifies

His Word on our behalf.

Read the next statement carefully—it is of supreme importance:

God clearly tells us what He will do for us in His Word, and from that point on, He deals with us on the basis of what we confess and do about His promises. A negative confession nullifies His Word on our behalf.

That is awesome! This is why He gave us His Word, because without His Word, there would be no way we could ever exercise faith to believe His promises. You cannot exercise faith in a vacuum. There has to be some object to set your faith on. In the case of God, it is His Word.

This is why Satan works so tenaciously to keep the Word of God out of the hands of the people, because he knows if they ever learn how to confess the Word, they will open the floodgates for God to move on their behalf. When this finally takes place, his season of dominating their lives will be over. No slaveholder likes to lose his slaves. In Mark 16:19-20, we see the importance of God's Word:

19 *So then, after the Lord had spoken to them,*
He was received up into heaven, and sat
down at the right hand of God.

20 *And they went out and preached everywhere,*
the Lord working with them and confirming
the word through the accompanying signs.
Amen.

Notice that it did not say Jesus confirmed them, the people, but He confirmed His Word. If there is no Word, God has nothing to confirm.

CHAPTER FIVE

OUT OF THE ABUNDANCE
OF THE HEART
THE MOUTH SPEAKS

T o show how important our words are, Jesus says in Matthew 12:34:

> *"Brood of vipers! How can you, being evil, speak*
>
> *good things? For out of the abundance of the*
>
> *heart the mouth speaks."*

This is awesome! *Death* and *life* are in the power of the tongue. Your heart is your spirit. This is the part of you that has been born again.

Jesus did not say . . . out of the abundance of the head. This is where we have missed it. We have been thinking we had to deal with God scientifically or academically. No! Jesus said, for out of the abundance of the heart (your spirit man), the mouth speaks.

Whatever is in your heart in abundance, that is what is going to come out of your mouth, and that, my dear precious friend, is what is going to control your life.

What do you have down there in your heart in abundance? Abundance means a whole lot. It means "mucho" or much. For out of the abundance of the heart the mouth speaks. In other words, my mouth cannot speak but what is in my heart. What is in there in abundance? What have you been programming into your heart in abundance?

Many have been born again. No questions about it, their names are written in the Lamb's Book of Life. They are children of God. If they were to die today, they would go to heaven, no question about it. However, what about this life? If all God wanted you to do was go to heaven, then the most natural thing that should happen as soon as you confess Christ as your personal Savior, is that you ought to drop dead so you can go right on to heaven. There is no point in hanging around here for 60 more years. What for? What are you going to do down here for 60 more years if God's plan is for you to go to heaven?

No, God's plan is for you to live here victoriously. Then, when you finish here, take a vacation and go on to heaven, because that is when you will be at rest. You will be sunning yourself on God's beaches. But for now, God wants us to live abundantly down here.

Jesus said, "I came . . . . " He did not say, I drew you up to heaven. He said, "I came that you might have life and have it more abundantly." He wants us to have abundant life. Not struggling. Not hard trials and tribulations. Not trying to claw your way up the back side of the mountain. Jesus said, "I came that you might have life and have it more abuntantly."

However, we will never experience that abundant life until we learn how to operate in the spiritual law of the power of positive confession.

Matthew 12:34-37:

34   *"Brood of vipers! How can you, being evil, speak good things? For out of the abundance of the heart the mouth speaks.*

35   *"A good man out of the good treasure of his heart brings forth good things, and an evil man out of the evil treasure brings forth evil things.*

36   *"But I say to you that for every idle word men may speak, they will give account of it in the day of judgment.*

37   *"For by your words you will be justified, and by your words you will be condemned."*

Notice what verse 37 does not say. It does not say for by your *works* you will be justified and by your *works* you will be condemned. No, Jesus said, "By your *words*." It is by the words of your mouth. That is awesome!

As Christians we should do the works of God. Because we know from the scriptures that by your works, you will get some rewards, or lose rewards if the works are not the works of God. However, Jesus said, "by your words, you will be justified." Justified means "declared righteous." This is how you got saved, by your mouth.

Romans 10:9-10 tell it like this:

9   *that if you confess [say] with your mouth the Lord Jesus and believe in your heart that*

69

God has raised Him from the dead, you will
he saved.

10 *For with the heart one believes unto righteousness,*
and with the mouth confession [speaking words]
is made unto salvation.

CHANGE YOUR WORDS!

Proverbs 18:21

Death and life are in the power of the tongue,
and those who love it will eat its fruit.

I have to let God's Word come out of my mouth to give God something to confirm in my life. If you do not like what has been happening in your life, then change your words. And, of course, your heart.

Do not blame the white folks, and do not blame the blacks in the ghetto. They are not your problem. Do not blame the communists over in another country, and do not blame the man in the moon or the Martians. Go look in the mirror when you are in the bathroom by yourself and the door is locked. The person you see in the mirror, that is your problem.

I do not know about you, but I am thrilled to find out that nobody can mess me up. Thank God, I am the one who decides. Not because it is me, but because God designed the system to work that way. For by *your* words . . ., Jesus said. Not, by *their* words.

What you say does not make any difference. Not when it comes to me and my personal life and relationship with God. Thank God, I am the only one who can mess me up. My wife cannot mess me up. My children cannot mess me up. No one can mess up my personal, individual life. When we do something corporately as a family, then they can hinder me. If we do something corporately as a church, then others can hinder me. But I can step out of that role and get over here in my own thing and the Lord and I can go for it! And I like that.

We cannot blame anyone else. If I mess up, that is me. I have to go ahead and admit, "I am the one who messed up." Some people are always giving alibis. "Well, if it wasn't for those folk down there; if it wasn't for the people over there; if it wasn't for the Democrats; if it wasn't for the Republicans." Stop! Take responsibility for yourself! You are the one. It's nobody else's fault, but yours.

It has nothing to do with where you were born. It has nothing to do with your mother, your father, your sister or your brother. It has nothing to do with anything but you and God, and you ought to thank God on a daily basis that that is the case. Thank Him that nobody can mess you up. If you are messed up, it is your own fault and not God's. You cannot blame anyone else, because with Jesus you can climb out of that pit.

I do not want to hear about how bad you had it. "Well, you just don't know how abused I was when I was a kid." The point of the matter is that you are no longer that kid. What is your excuse now? Besides that, that abuse is under the blood of Jesus and that blood will cleanse you of any and all abuse. If you will do what His Word says, casting all your care upon Him, for He cares for you (1 Peter 5:7), then it will not rise up to threaten you or be a specter in the dark of night to frighten you while you are in your bed alone.

I do not care what they did. They could have raped you, beat you on the head and done every manner of evil to you. This has nothing to do with the power of the blood of Jesus. It has nothing to do with the fact that you are a child of the Most High God right now. Stop copping out with all that junk of the past. The past means nothing—it is over. It is done. No, it should not have happened. No, your father should not have molested you, but he did and it is over now. Forget it, and go forward. Stop living in the past. It will do you no good to dwell on past evils.

Philippians 3:13-14 say:

13   *Brethren, I do not count myself to have apprehended; but one thing I do, forgetting those things which are behind and reaching forward to those things which are ahead,*

14   *I press toward the goal for the prize of the upward call of God in Christ Jesus.*

What happened to you should never have happened. They should not have done that, but they did, and your thinking about it and carrying it to your grave is not going to change it. Put it under your feet. Bury that garbage. Forget it and get a hold of the Word of God.

Let the Word get down in your heart so that there is abundance there, so that when you open your mouth, out comes the Word of God and then God will confirm that in your life.

Yes, your first marriage was a disaster, but so what? It is over. You made a mistake. Forget about it. Get on with the rest of your life.

You may say, "I don't have any confidence in men. I don't trust men. They are all alike." You are lying! I rebuke that. All men are not alike. Just because you got a hold of a rat, do not think every man is a rat. "Men ain't no good. Honey, don't trust no man!" I have news for you. It was a man Who redeemed you. Better watch your mouth.

It is a Man sitting at the right hand of God interceding on your behalf. It is a Man Who loved you. It is a man Who exalted you to a station of life that has respect, and it is a Man Who is coming back to receive you to Himself. Watch your mouth.

Put your past behind you and start letting the Word of God come out of your mouth. Hide His Word down in your heart. God will confirm it in your life. Then nobody and nothing can stop you.

Circumstances cannot do a thing
to me without my consent.

I want to ask you a question: Who do you think determines whether or not you enjoy the full rich life of health, peace and prosperity that God promised in His Word?

Most people would answer, "God," but human experience does not bear that out. Some Christians are well and others are sick. Some have abundance while others struggle economically and materially. Some die young and are cut off in the prime of life, while others live out a long and full life. No, it could not be God.

Could it be Satan, better known as the devil? James 4:7 says this:

Therefore submit to God. Resist the
devil and he will flee from you.

How do you submit yourself to God? By submitting yourself to His Word. For God and His Word are one. When you submit to God's Word, you are submitting to God. According to God's Word, we can resist the devil and he must flee from us. That being true, then the devil could have nothing at all to do with whether we succeed or fail, live in wealth or lack. If not the devil, who?

I repeat the question: Who do you think determines whether or not you enjoy the full rich life of health, peace and prosperity that God promised in His Word?

The scriptures tell us it is not God or the devil. Then who could it be? Could it be circumstances? Whatever will be, will be. Maybe it is circumstances? No! Circumstances merely give you the opportunity to reveal the extent of your faith in God's Word. Circumstances cannot do a thing to me without my consent. Circumstances in and of themselves cannot cause victory or defeat. It is my response to the circumstances that determines what influence they will have on my life.

Matthew 17:20 gives us insight into this principle:

> So Jesus said to them, *"Because of your unbelief;*
> *for assuredly, I say to you, if you have faith as a*
> *mustard seed, you will say to this mountain,*
> *'Move from here to there,' and it will move; and*
> *nothing will be impossible for you."*

Jesus is speaking in this passage. Is He lying?

There was a man who brought his demonized child to the disciples and the disciples did not cast out the demon. Jesus was on the Mount of Transfiguration. When He came on the scene, He cast the demon out. After the man and his boy left, the disciples came to Jesus and asked, "Why could we not cast him out?" And Jesus said, in essence, that it was not the circumstances, but, rather, because of their unbelief.

In Matthew 17:14-16, we learn something very important:

14   *And when they had come to the multitude, a*
      man came to Him, kneeling down to Him and
      saying,

15   *"Lord, have mercy on my son, for he is*
      an epileptic and suffers severely; for he
      often falls into the fire and often into the
      water.

16   *"So I brought him to Your disciples, but*
      they could not cure him."

The man said they *could not* cure him—meaning either they did not have the power or the authority to do it. If that is true, then the father was a fool. For why would you bring your child to someone who had no power or ability to cure him? The real problem was the man's interpretation of the circumstances. The father's assessment of the situation was invalid. He said they *could not,* when literally, what he should have said was that they *did not.*

There has to be something in that man's experience that indicated that these disciples could help him; otherwise, he was foolish to bring his child to someone that he did not have any faith in. He had either heard about or seen the disciples do something, and it had inspired him to believe that they could help his child. For some reason, it did not work this time. Therefore, the father's interpretation was that they *could not.*

However, there is a difference between *could not* and *did not.* Jesus responded and said in Matthew 17:17-19,

17   . . . *"O faithless* [O what? Faithless! Do you know what faithless means? It means less faith.] *and perverse generation, how long shall I be with you?* [or put up with you] *How long shall I bear with you? Bring him here to Me."*

18   *And Jesus rebuked the demon, and it came out of him; and the child was cured from that very hour.*

19   *Then the disciples came to Jesus privately and said, "Why could we not cast it out?"*

There is a revelation here: If they did not have either the authority or the ability to cast that demon out, would they have known that?

I would never ask the question, "Why could I not get pregnant and have a baby?" I know why. I am not supposed to. I am not constructed that way. I could not if I wanted to, so I would never ask the question.

When they said, "Why could we not cast it out?" that very question indicated that they knew they had the authority and the ability, but for some reason, it did not work this time and so they said, "Why could we not do it?" If they had not been given the authority, the power and or ability to do it, would they not have known that?

The point I am making here is that you can have the authority and you can have the ability and still botch it up. Just because you are not abundantly supplied, do not assume that it is not the will of God for you to have it simply because you have not been experiencing it. Maybe the problem is you. Just like in the case of the disciples.

Jesus did not say, because you do not have the authority; He did not say, because you don't have the ability. He said, Because of your unbelief. Even though you have been delegated the authority and the ability, you can still operate in unbelief.

Let me show you the scripture that proves they had the authority. This is the reason why the father brought his epileptic son to them. Matthew 10:1 says:

> And when He had called His twelve disciples to Him, He gave them power [in the Greek, the word "power" is exousia, which literally means authority] over unclean spirits, to cast them out, and to heal all kinds of sickness and all kinds of disease.

Jesus gave the disciples authority to cast them out, but they did not do it. That is the same thing that is happening to the Church today. Almost 2,000 years ago, Jesus Christ, the Head of the Church, gave to the Church, His Body, the authority to cast out demons; the authority to speak with new tongues; the authority to lay hands on the sick so they would recover; the authority to be victorious in life; and yet the Church has been whipped, defeated and not carrying out the great commission that God gave us.

We have assumed that it was not the will of God and yet, He gave the disciples that authority and He also gave it to us. However, authority that is not exercised will do no one any good. All the authority does is give you the right to do something, but you still have to do it. The authority does not do it, *you* do it.

If you are not enjoying the full, rich life in Christ, do not blame God, do not blame the devil, and do not blame the circumstances. Go look in the mirror. You are the problem. Raise your right hand, make a finger, put it on the tip of your nose and say, "I'm the one!" You are the one! I thank God for that, because it puts us all on par. Nobody has any advantage over anyone else.

Let's see what Jesus has to say in Matthew 21:21-22 about this matter:

> 21 . . . *"Assuredly, I say to you, if you have faith and do not doubt, you will not only do what was done to the fig tree, but also if you say to this mountain, 'Be removed and be cast into the sea,' it will be done.*
>
> 22 *"And whatever things you ask in prayer, believing, you will receive."*

WHAT YOU THINK, BELIEVE & CONFESS PRECONDITIONS YOUR LIFE

Remember this principle: *Everyone preconditions his life by what he thinks, by what he believes, and by what he confesses.* Remember what we read in Proverbs 18:21: Death and life are in the power of the tongue . . . . Hebrews 3:1 says, *Therefore, holy brethren, partakers of the heavenly calling, consider the Apostle and High Priest of our confession, Christ Jesus.*

Jesus is our High Priest. How? He is the High Priest of our confession. In other words, Jesus is the High Priest of our words. Jesus presides over our words. As our High Priest, Jesus can act on our behalf, to save, bless, heal, protect and deliver—provided we give Him a positive confession which is in harmony with the Word of God. A confession of doubt, a confession of fear concerning our circumstances or our situation in life, hinders His ministry on our behalf.

Consider these confessions:

"Well, brother, sister, how are you doing today?"

"Well, I'm just barely makin' it." or

"Oh, I think I'm going to be sick." or

"Well, I hear there's a very very strong case of the flu

comin' on. I'll probably get it because I always do."

These kinds of confessions are said all the time, and most people never think anything about it. Jesus cannot act as the High Priest of these kinds of confessions, because these confessions are inconsistent with the Word of God. You said you are probably going to be sick. You said, you are probably going to get the flu, and the Bible says, "With His stripes, you were healed." Did you get that? The Bible said, "With His stripes you were healed."

The scriptures clearly show us that sickness, health, poverty, prosperity, or adversities are directly related to our confessions—to our words! A confession of doubt or fear concerning our situation hinders the ministry of Jesus our High Priest on our behalf and opens a channel of access for Satan to come in like a flood to destroy and oppress.

I want to use sickness as an illustration, because that is one of the areas in which God uses me, ministering to the sick. I would like to share with you a threefold principle. I want you to follow this carefully, because it will not only help you individually, but it will help you to help others whom you love. It will help you to understand why some that you have known, some that you have loved that had a genuine commitment to God and to Christ became sick and died of that sickness. Some people said, God caused their death or illness: "The Lord took them." Others said, "God works in mysterious ways, His wonders to perform."

Most of the time, we do not know what is in the heart of another person. We really do not know what their attitude is concerning God's Word. They may be very nice people, love the Lord, and have had a genuine experience of salvation or conversion. Yet they may not know the Word of God, or they may not be committed to the Word. They may have read the Word, they may have heard it, but they are not really living it. Many people are like that. Perhaps even you!

When illness strikes, when sickness comes there are three things you must consider if you are to receive healing. The first thing that you must know is: What does God say about my condition? The symptoms say you are sick. The thermometer says you are sick. However, what does God say?

Let me make this very clear, because I do not want anybody to go off and mess up on this: If the thermometer says that you have a temperature of 105, you have in the natural a temperature of 105. I am not denying that, but you see, you have a choice. You can either go with what the symptoms tell you, or you can go with what God tells you. Now that is an awesome choice. Again, I do not deny that the thermometer says 105. This is not what is important to me. What is important is what does God say about that 105 degree temperature?

You have to be absolutely, positively, unequivocally committed to the Word of God. You have to believe without any shadow of doubt that what God says about your condition is so. If you have to ask the question, if you have to think, "Well what if . . . ." forget it! Go with the thermometer. Do not waste any time;

you could die. You have to be completely and totally sold out to the Word of God, and everybody is not there yet. This is all right. This is not a putdown. It is not meant to be a condemnation. There is a place in God where you can rise up and live in victory every day, but it is going to cost you a total commitment, a sellout. Only you can know if you are really "sold out."

Whenever you are uncertain and say things like, "What about . . .?" or "Maybe . . ." you are not there yet, so do not play around with it. If your temperature is 105, you better do what the doctor tells you to do to get it down from 105, because you cannot last long with a temperature of 105. However, this is what God says about your condition in Psalm 103:3:

> *Who forgives all your iniquities, Who heals*
> *all your diseases.*

Taking a stand on God's Word means you must say, "God has healed the fever of 105, and I now believe I receive my healing." When you make this confession of faith, you might start feeling worse. Your temperature may go up to 106, so you have to be ready to take a stand, or else Satan will intimidate you. Every time you say, "I believe I receive . . . " the devil will say, "Boo!" — all designed to frighten you. However, you have to be committed. You have to be sold out to what God says or it will not work.

Satan Will Try to Intimidate You

The next thing you need to know if you are going to receive your healing is: What does Satan say about my condition? There are no specific Bible verses for this, but I will tell you how he operates against you. The devil will work through your senses and mind. He will oppress you in the realm of the senses and then right on the heels of that he will send a negative thought to your mind.

Have you ever awakened in the morning and stepped out of bed and suddenly a pain hits you in a certain part of your body? You did not go to bed with that pain. You did not dream about that pain, and you were not expecting or looking for any pain. The pain hit you maybe in the back, leg, arm, or shoulder. Then almost instantly, a thought comes to your mind, "You're getting arthritis, or bursitis." Or, "You are going to have a coronary."

Who do you think that came from? Do you think the Holy Spirit put that in your mind? No! This is the way Satan works. He sends negative thoughts like, "You are going to be sick. That sharp pain you had in your breast must be cancer. After all, Grandma died from that." Now when those kinds of thoughts come, you have to be convinced that when the Word of God says, Who heals all your diseases, it is talking about you.

Instantly you have to speak to that pain in Jesus' name. You cannot wait around. If you let fear come in, then you need to get some help fast, because you are in trouble. You have to stand against it in faith. It does not mean that you do not seek medical help to assist you in terms of the symptoms. Pain is symptomatic. Pain is not a cause of anything. God built the body system so that it would give alerts when something goes wrong. Pain is an alert system. If you grabbed something that was 125 degrees hot and you had no sensation in your hand, you could burn your hand off, and you would not know it. However, as soon as you touch it, the alert system goes into effect.

Therefore, you may need something, perhaps medication, to deal with that pain, or whatever is wrong with you, so that you can continue to function. Your faith should not be in the medication because that is not going to heal you anyway. The power of God will do it. Because if that medication could heal you, everyone that took the medication would be healed and we know that this is not the case. No, God will work through the doctors and medication, but ultimately He is the one Who provides divine healing.

Some people have languished on beds of affliction for years, pumped full of medications and still died from the condition. My mother-in-law, who is now deceased, is a case in point. She had acute arthritis for more than 20 years. She had taken so much medication during those 20 years that it had almost destroyed her body. She did not look like a human. She needed it to survive, and thank God for it. However, if the medication could heal, she should have been healed after 20 years of medication. Medication has its place, and it can deal with symptoms until the power of God removes the cause.

Do not let anyone put you in bondage about taking medication. Satan will tell you, "You are going to be sick. You feel that pain? Remember your mother-in-law died of that." If you listen to that, you begin to think it, say it, and fear comes in. This will open the door for Satan to put the sickness on you. "Well, after all, it runs in the family." Nothing runs in my family but divine health. I am not accepting anything less! I do not care how often it comes, I believe I am well. In fact, I believe that I walk in divine health. This is my personal and daily confession of faith. You have to make a choice to speak what God says about you.

The *third* thing you need to know, if you are going to receive your healing is: What do I say about my condition? There are three things you must know. (1) What does God say? (2) What does Satan say? (3) What do you say? Whatever you say is going to either legitimize what God says, or what the devil says. You are the one who decides whether the battle swings to God or to the devil. You are in control. Your confession is what will make the difference. Keep in mind that you cannot say anything if you do not know what God has already said about your situation in His Word. If you have not made a commitment to say what God says about it, you are in serious trouble.

Read this very carefully because it could save your life: Do not make the fatal mistake of saying what you would like your condition to be. You must say what you actually believe in your heart. Because if you don't, you could die while you are waiting for what you would like it to be, to come up to what you actually are able to believe it to be.

If you ask people, "Do you believe you are healed?" They will usually respond, "Well, I certainly want to believe that, Brother Price." That person is not in faith. That is what they would like, and that is fine. They ought to want that, but this will not work with you wanting that to be so, you have to believe it right now. You cannot afford to gamble with your life.

The moment the symptom shows up, you have to stand against the symptom then. You have to pounce on it like a dog on a bone. You have to get on it like a cat with a canary and say, "I believe, according to the Word of God, that I am healed from the top of my head to the soles of my feet, I am well in the name of Jesus." You have to do that instantly.

There are many of you who want the things that God has to offer. However, you are not able to truly say, "I believe I receive." No more discussion of the subject. I believe I am well. I believe my need is met now. If you are not convinced right now, then get some help quickly. You cannot afford to wait around.

Do you understand what I am saying? You have to be convinced right now! The way you do this is to start using your faith on little, infinitesimal, insignificant things that do not amount to a hill of beans. Things that are not terminal. Things that are not crises. The little every day things that ordinarily you would not even have to use any faith on. This is what you practice on.

Do not wait until you have terminal cancer to practice faith. Do not wait until the marshal is walking up to the door to foreclose on and evict you from your house. It is too late then. Do you understand that? Do not wait until some major crisis occurs and then start saying, "I believe I receive."

This is an example of how you may begin to practice developing your faith: You may have enough money to buy a suit of clothes. Do not buy the suit of clothes with the money. Do not charge it to the charge account. Take the charge card, get the cash for the cost of the suit, and send it as a seed of faith to a ministry. Then believe God and use your faith for that suit. If the suit never comes, it does not affect your life and you have not lost a thing. You can always go back and buy it. Do you understand that? However, that is an example of how you can begin to learn to walk by faith. This is called, "on-the-job training."

WHAT DO YOU SAY ABOUT YOUR CONDITION?

What do you say about your condition? What you say will have to be based on what you believe, which should be based on what God says in His Word. Brother, sister, you have to be convinced. This is not a gambling situation. This is not lotto, a kind of "maybe you will and maybe you will not" game. If you do not know, then do something else until you do know.

Do you feel ashamed about your faith level? You do not need to be ashamed. It is the wise man who recognizes his limitations and then does something about it. It is the fool who goes on, oblivious to what he is not able to do, thinking he is going to do it anyway and gets his head broken. Do not do that.

What does God say? What does the devil say? And what do you say? You are the one who decides what is going to prevail in your life. Your confession will line up with what God says, or it will line up with what the devil says. Whichever one it lines up with, guess what? That is what you are going to have in life. If you keep the umbrella of God's protection up, you can walk right through the storm, and come out dry. If you do not observe to do His Word, the curses, which are already there, will come upon you. This means you do not have God's umbrella up—you have no protection.

Now I want to show you something else. This should help some of you who have been sitting around all your Christian life nursing some ailment like arthritis, bursitis, heart condition, varicose veins, or whatever it might be. You have been nursing that thing, thinking you are suffering for the Lord, not realizing you were suffering because you are ignorant—ignorant of God's Word. Look at Deuteronomy 28:61:

> *Also every sickness and every plague, which is not written in this Book of the Law, will the LORD bring* [permit to be brought] *upon you until you are destroyed.*

In verses 20-28 of this same chapter the Bible talks about all kinds of diseases that affect every part of your body. This passage says, God will send or bring upon you things that are not even written in the Book. The way it is worded in these verses, it looks like God is doing the cursing. However, the translation is incorrect. These verses should have been rendered, "the Lord will permit."

What I am saying is that you have been nursing your condition, thinking you were serving God, thinking that God wanted you to hold on and keep a stiff upper lip, and always praise Him right in the middle of all that sickness and disease. However, you ought to be able to tell by this information that sickness and disease are not from God and it is not His will for you to suffer.

CHAPTER SIX

SATAN, OUR ADVERSARY; JESUS, OUR ADVOCATE

Revelation 12:10:

Then I heard a loud voice saying in heaven, "Now salvation, and strength, and the kingdom of our God, and the power of His Christ have come, for the accuser of our brethren, who accused them before our God day and night, has been cast down. "

This is why you have to be "on the job," friend. You have an adversary who works day and night. You do not stand a chance to win if you letdown your guard. This opponent is out to get you. He wants you dead! We can be dead in the sense of not being able to combat him with the Word of God and the power of the Holy Spirit.

Think about it: he is accusing you day and night! What do you think he is accusing you with? Words. In other words, he is talking you down. Satan is a legalist. When it comes to us, he will use the letter of the law against us, so we need help and God has provided that help.

God has provided a public defender Who is above reproach. In fact, God has provided a public defender Who has been taught the law by the Judge of all ages. Nobody knows the law better than Jesus, and the public that He defends is the public of the Kingdom of God and that is us.

In 1 John 2:1, it says:

> *My little children, these things I write to you, so that you may not sin. And if anyone sins, we have an Advocate with the Father, Jesus Christ the righteous.*

The word *advocate* is a legal term. In the Greek, this word has reference to a courtroom scene. Literally, it means counsel for the defense. Satan stands before the throne of God accusing the brethren day and night. The high tribunal of God is open 24 hours a day, every day of the week. There is never a holiday and thank God for that!

Hebrews 3:1 tells us that Jesus is the High Priest of our confession. If you combine His high priestly function with His legal function, then He becomes the counsel for our defense, and at the same time, the High Priest of our confession.

Unlike earthly lawyers, this counsel for the defense cannot be intimidated, nor can He be bought. This counsel for the defense is not going to be concerned with whether you are able to pay a fee or not. In fact, the services of this law firm are given to the citizens of this kingdom without charge.

How does this counsel for our defense defend us in the high tribunal of heaven when we have an adversary, the accuser of the brethren who is accusing us day and night? He defends us on the basis of two things: (1) He provides intercession and (2) we provide our confession. If we do not provide ours, we throw the case to the prosecuting attorney (Satan) and we will be convicted. However, if we can bring our evidence, our attorney has irrefutable evidence. By putting His evidence together with ours, it is an open-and-shut case in our favor, and we are set free.

Look at Revelation 12:10-11:

> 10 *Then I heard a loud voice saying in heaven, "Now salvation, and strength, and the kingdom of our God, and the power of His Christ have come, for the accuser of our brethren, who accused them before our God day and night, has been cast down.*
>
> 11 *"And they overcame him by the blood of the Lamb and by the word of their testimony, and they did not love their lives to the death."*

This is how Jesus defends us, on the basis of His shed blood. And guess what? On the word of our testimony! Whether you realize it or not, that word *testimony* is another word for confession.

Let me say it again: The way Jesus defends us is on the basis of His shed blood and our confession. If I do not make a confession that is consistent with the Word of God, Jesus does not have anything to defend me with. Then, the prosecuting attorney, the accuser of the brethren (Satan), can make a case stick against me, because I am saying what Satan is saying. When I say what Satan says about me it makes me look like I am exactly what he says I am—guilty as charged. We have to learn how to say what our Father says about us so that we can bring our confession in line with Jesus' shed blood, and then we win.

91

Jesus is pleading our defense against Satan's accusations, not only with His precious blood, but also with our testimony — what we say! When I say, "I think I am going to be sick," I am not giving Jesus a testimony with which He can defend me, because it is contrary to the revealed Word of God. The Judge can only uphold the law, which is His Word.

When I discovered this and looked back on my life, I said, "No wonder I was in court every day! No wonder I was always getting sentenced. I never said anything in line with what Jesus could defend me with. And the churches I went to never told me that I had any defense anyway. In fact, they told me God was my problem. I did not realize that I had a prosecuting attorney who was trying to put me behind bars for life. However, thank God I have an Advocate, but I have to give Jesus my words. Words that are consistent with God's Word. When I do that, Jesus will defend me. If you join your confession with the words of your adversary, then Jesus cannot act as your High Priest. You tie His hands.

If an attorney, such as a public defender, has a client and the client gets in court and says, "I'm guilty, I'm guilty. I killed him. I shot him six times right between the eyes!" there is not much the attorney can do to defend that client. Likewise, when we make a confession that is inconsistent with the revealed Word of God, it is like saying, "I killed him, I killed him!" We negate our counsel's ability to defend us.

CHAPTER SEVEN

AFFIRMING BIBLICAL TRUTHS RESULTS IN LIVING VICTORIOUSLY

L_{et} us now consider some important biblical principles, which can determine how victorious you will be in your Christian walk. The victorious Christian life is based upon a positive confession of four basic biblical truths. A positive affirmation of the following four truths will compel Satan to acknowledge our authority and our victory over him. This will in turn break the enemy's power to successfully bind, hinder, and oppress you.

God expects us to confess:

(1) What We Are in Christ

(2) Where We Are in Christ

(3) What We Possess in Christ

(4) What We Can Do in Christ

When you get a revelation of these four things, you are on your way to the top. You are on your way to victorious Christian living. You are on your way to living the kind of life that Christ gave His life for.

Christ did not give up His life for you to be defeated. He did not give up His life for you to be walked on like a doormat. Christ did not come down here and defeat death, hell, the grave, Satan, and every demon for you to be laid up on some bed of affliction for 25 years. This was not why He came. Jesus could have remained in heaven and you would have still had the curse. Although the vast majority of Christians are experiencing a whipped and defeated lifestyle, and because God does not reach down supernaturally and change it, they think that their situation must be the will of God. They fail to realize, because they have never been taught, that it is not up to God, it is up to us, whether we live defeated or victorious.

In Matthew 18:18, Jesus says:

> *Assuredly, I say to you, whatever you bind on*
> *earth will be bound in heaven, and whatever you*
> *loose on earth will be loosed in heaven.*

Notice that the word *earth* comes before the word *heaven* in each one of the statements. Notice that the binding and loosening starts on earth. It does not start in heaven and come down to earth. This lets me know that it is my choice, that I have something to do with it, and that thrills me.

In the following chapters of this book, we will look at these four biblical truths in detail and learn how to apply them to our lives.

CHAPTER EIGHT

FACT 1A:

WHAT WE ARE IN CHRIST

We must confess *what we are in Christ* if we expect to live the victorious Christian life. This statement refers to your stand with God. According to God's Word, you are everything God says you are, whether you are presently experiencing it or not. If you are not living up to God's level, that is your problem, not His. If you are not what God says you are, then God lied. If God lied about that, how do you know what part of His Word is the truth and what part is a lie? You do not. Either it is all a lie or it is all the truth.

When I was saved and began attending church, I was not told how I stood with God. The only thing I was told was that I was just a sinner saved by grace. How could I confess what I did not know?

I want to go through the scriptures and point you to a few choice statements, the kind that I would encourage you to search out for yourself. This will be a starter course, so that you can get an idea of what you should be confessing. We must confess God's Word if we are to overcome the onslaught of defeatism that the enemy has brought, and will continue to bring against us to prevent us from living a victorious Christian life.

God wants you to be a winner. Whether you realize it or not, God only operates with winning. There is no defeat in God, even though for years we have been sold a bill of goods by those who supposedly represented Him. They told us, "Sometimes up and sometimes down, and sometimes almost level to the ground." However, this is not in the Bible. We are winners just like the Word of God says we are.

In 2 Corinthians 5:17, we have a very familiar verse, but a verse very important to us as Christians.

> *Therefore, if anyone is in Christ, he is a new creation; old things have passed away; behold, all things have become new.*

We understand when He talks about "anyone," He is including both males and females. If anyone is in Christ . . . , how does a person get in Christ? By being born again. In other words, by doing what Romans 10:9 says,

> *that if you confess with your mouth the Lord Jesus and believe in your heart that God has raised Him from the dead, you will be saved.*

If you have done this, then you are in Christ and Christ is in you and you are "a new creation." You were originally a creation of God, but now you are a new creation. What does "new" tell you? It refers to something that has never been before. This is what God says you are—something that you have never been before.

Let me, however, qualify a few things in this verse. It says . . . *old things have passed away*. If old things have passed away, that means the old things no longer exist. Is that a fair estimate? It further states, *behold, all things have become new*. We have to define what the old things that passed away are and what all the things that have become new are. In that way, we can pinpoint where we are old and where we are new, so that we will know how to relate to what God says about us.

ONLY YOUR SPIRIT IS NEW

Right away, if you are not careful, you will naturally assume that this is talking about being a brand-new person all over. If I am a brand-new person all over, then that means I am brand-new physically. In most churches, we have not been told that we are more than flesh and blood. We have heard the word *soul*, but we did not know what it meant.

We would assume that if we are a new creation, then we are new in our bodies, but we are not. There is nothing new about your body—it is the same body you had before being saved. I submit to you that the physical part of you did not pass away, and that all things did not become new in your body.

Here is my proof: if old things passed away in your physical body, it would mean that if you had false teeth before you got saved should have a brand-new set of natural teeth in your mouth now, and you know that is not true. If you were baldheaded the day before you got saved, you still have no hair on your cranial cavity the day after. The point I am making, and I am not trying to be funny, is that physically, we are the same.

When a woman gives birth to a baby, physically her body goes through a traumatic change. Likewise, there is something that happens to you spiritually when you are born again. You feel highly exhilarated. When you come in contact with God and Christ, it is a joyous, almost unexplainable experience. It affects your whole being and it is awesome.

The woman who gives birth to the baby goes through a traumatic experience, but it does come to an end. When the baby is birthed, it is over, and then she returns to what is called normalcy. In like manner, when you are born again, you go through a spiritual birth experience, but it comes to an end and you settle back into a normalcy; only this time, it ought to be a normalcy in the framework of the Word of God.

This is the area where many people miss it. Because when you first come in contact with Christ, it is so exhilarating, so thrilling, and so wonderful that you think you are going to stay like that the rest of your life. However, that state of exhilaration was never designed to last indefinitely, any more than it was designed for a woman, once she gives birth to stay in the same state of giving birth for the next 20 years.

When you go through the new birth, your spirit becomes new. God puts a brand-new spirit in you. After you experience the trauma of the new birth, you settle back into a normal mode of living, except this normalcy ought to be spiritually motivated based on God's Word. If you do not know this, you will return to living as you were before you ever came in contact with Jesus. Your physical body will end up governing you and directing you. Your old mind that has not yet been renewed by the Word of God will gravitate back to doing the same things you used to do, thinking the same things you used to think. The only difference is you will start feeling a twinge of conscience when you do those fleshy things. You know that something is wrong, and you should not have done it, but you did it, and somehow you feel like you cannot help yourself.   When you were made new, only your spirit was made new — these are the old things that passed away.

In your spirit, before you became a Christian, you were alienated and separated from God. You were in a state of what is called "spiritual death," a state of "sin consciousness." After you receive Jesus, you are no longer alienated and separated from God. You no longer have spiritual death abiding in you. You are now a new creation in Christ Jesus. You now have the life of God in you and your past, spiritually speaking, is over.

Since I am a new creation, I have to guard my mouth so that I do not say what Satan attempts to infiltrate into my unrenewed mind about who I used to be, to get me to return to that former level of existence. Satan wants to get me back to my former negative actions and confessions.

If you do not guard yourself, your old mind, which has not yet been renewed by the Word of God, will gravitate back to doing the same things you used to do and thinking the same things you used to think. The only difference is you will start feeling a twinge of conscience when you do those things. You know that you should not be doing them, but somehow you feel as though you cannot help yourself.

God said I am a new creation. I need to stand in front of the mirror of my life and say, "Praise God, I am a brand-new creation. I am not what I used to be; therefore, I must seek new levels of operation, because I am no longer the person that I used to be. I cannot see myself that way anymore." I may have to change my so-called friends. This goes for any born-again believer. You may have to make a new list of friends and a new list of places to go because there is a new person on the inside. God's design is that my spirit man feed on the Word of God so that my re-created spirit will direct and change my mind or soul, and bring my body in line with God's Word.

The devil knows that once we Christians are empowered with the Word we will be able to keep him out of our lives. This is the reason he has very cleverly kept most Christians from reading and studying the Bible. He does not mind you going to church. He does not mind you whooping and and hollering; he does not mind you singing loud and making a lot of noise, because there is no life in that.

You have churches full of people who love the Lord, and have had a genuine experience with God, but their bodies control, dominate, and direct their lives. My body controlled me, too, until I found out how to control it. I thought all those cravings I had were normal. I said, "I am just doing what comes naturally," I thought. Naturally sinning, naturally messing up, naturally doing what was wrong.

I did not understand. I thought my body was new, until I found out that my physical body was not a part of me that got born again. I now keep my body under lock and key. I do not trust my body. I never let it out ot my sight. Your body is not what is saved. We, as Christians, live our lives in a physical context, but it should be spiritually motivated.

Now, *if anyone is in Christ, he is a new creation; old things have passed away; behold, all things have become new.* This is who God says I am. I am a new creation. I cannot lie anymore. I cannot steal anymore because God said I am new. When the devil comes with his temptation, I say, "No, I can't do that, devil, because I am new." If you still think you are the same old wretch that you used to be, what do you expect a wretch to do but mess up? Therefore, it is very easy to gravitate back to sin. As the Bible says about the dog: he returns to his vomit. He does not know any better. However, you know better, because you are a new creation in Christ Jesus.

You are everything that God says you are. This is what the statement "we walk by faith and not by sight" means. I use that scripture all the time. When you walk by faith, it simply means you walk by what God says in His Word. This principle seems so hard for most Christians to understand. They still let their emotions (their soul), and bodies (their flesh), get involved. God's Word is what should direct my life, and it is by faith that I do it.

I have to ignore signals from my body and thoughts from my mind. I have to operate strictly by what the Word says. If I do not, I will be messed up and so will you. You will be on the "yo-yo syndrome"—up one day and down the next. You certainly do not want to be that way. You should want to be constant, but you will never be constant unless you operate by faith.

It is for this reason that I harp on faith all the time. Thirty-years ago the Lord impressed upon me that faith is the key to everything. In essence, the Lord said, "Fred, if you ever get faith into your spirit where it becomes the watchword of your life, you will be able to master and overcome everything that ever attempts to come against you. You can never be defeated, if you learn to walk by faith."

If you walk by the situations of life, if you walk by what your body tells you, you will be constantly in flux, constantly changing. There are all kinds of things Satan will throw against you to affect your body. He will trick you into thinking that if a thought comes into your mind, that means you thought it up and so it is just as bad to think it, as it is to do it. Since you thought it, you might as well go ahead and do it. This is a lie right out of the pit of hell! Do not fall for that garbage.

I do not care what kind of thoughts come in your mind, do not get into a guilt trip when those thoughts come. I am not telling you to sit around all day thinking about pornography. Negative thoughts come to everyone, but the issue is, what do you do with them? You have to resist that negative thought and you can do it because you are new, and none of that old behavior is in the new spiritual creation.

If you were walking down the street and saw a pile of cow manure, you would not have any problems resisting the temptation to go pick it up and have it for lunch. You may say, "That is gross!" But so are fornication, oral sex, homosexuality, lesbianism, alcoholism, and drugs. If you develop that kind of attitude—that sin is gross like that cow manure—you will keep your hands off. In fact, to get right down to it, it would do you better to eat cow manure than to suck on cancer sticks (cigarettes) or snort cocaine.

This is the kind of attitude you ought to have about all those sinful things out there. Treat them like the Bible says, like dung, manure. I do not have a problem resisting manure, do you?

Would you pull the sheets back on a bed and lie down on a mattress of cow manure? Well, when you are tempted to get in bed with someone who is not your spouse, see that bed as cow manure and you will put your clothes on and get out of that place!

I would wager that there are some reading this book right now, who wish they had thought about that years ago. Some are paying right now for things they did 25 years ago. They wish to God they had thought of it as cow manure, and then they would not be in the mess they are today.

WE ARE COMPLETE IN HIM

Colossians 2:9-10:

> 9 *For in Him dwells all the fullness of the Godhead bodily;*

> 10 *and you are complete in Him, who is the head of all principality and power.*

You are what? What does *complete* mean? It means "entire or whole." If you are complete — whole — then you are lacking nothing. How can I be complete in Him, and have an inferiority complex? If I am complete in Him, how can I have low self-esteem? We have been listening to the devil's lie far too long, instead of listening to God's Word, which tells us that we are complete.

When you begin to see yourself as complete and begin to confess that, speaking life to your life, it will cause you to live up to what God says about you. It is not a psych job. It is releasing the power of God, and the power of God is released by the words that we speak. We just read it. The Word of God said, "We are complete in Christ." If we are not complete in Christ, then

God lied to us and the Bible says He cannot lie, so we must be complete.

We need to see ourselves as God sees us. We are complete in Christ, which is the head of all principality and power. We are in Christ, so we are complete. When people do not understand that, they will think you are arrogant. They will think you are a braggart, braggadocious, self-centered. However, you cannot be intimidated by that. You have to know and confess who God says you are.

You are whole in Christ. There is nothing left out of you. When God gave you that new re-created human spirit, there was no shortage in it. You have to see yourself as a new creation, and then you will begin to think and talk about yourself God's way. All of a sudden you will find yourself acting as a new person who demonstrates the righteousness of Christ. You will begin to act in character with the way Jesus would act.

A dog barks because it is a dog. This is the language of a dog. You do not hear dogs mooing. It is not their nature. It is natural for a dog to bark, for a cat to meow, and for a cow to moo because that is their nature. Well, you have the nature of God, and in that nature there is completeness.

I am a whole person in God. Now, that does not mean that I do not have to work on sharpening myself up, but rather that I have all of the necessary ingredients to be like Jesus. There is nothing that is left out, and if I will keep mixing the "cake-mix" with my tongue, in terms of confessing who I am, I will finally get the batter—my life—just the way it is supposed to be. I will have a beautiful cake with icing and candles on top!

I have to see myself that way and say that about myself, and not let anybody tell me who I am or what I am. I am what God says I am, and I say what God says, so I am what I say I am. It does not matter to me what you think. It does not move me in the least. Think whatever you want. I am not what I am because of what you or anyone else thinks. I am complete because God says I am.

Colossians 1:12-13:

12   *giving thanks to the Father who has qualified us* [which means able] *to be partakers of the inheritance of the saints in the light.*

13   *He has delivered us from the power of darkness and conveyed us into the kingdom of the Son of His love,*

In verse 13, the word *has* is used. This is a past-tense designation. It indicates that the time of action has already taken place. It is not in the process of taking place, or in the future; it is already done. This is exciting to me . . . *has delivered us* . . . . Make the Word of God personal: *who has delivered me.* This means every one of us. He told me He has delivered me. What have we been delivered from? That word *power* means the authority or dominion of darkness.

The word *darkness* in this scripture does not mean nighttime. It is talking about the kingdom of Satan. It tells us in the same verse that we have been translated into the kingdom of His dear Son. You are in somebody's kingdom all the time. You are either in the kingdom of light or the kingdom of darkness — God's kingdom or Satan's kingdom.

Since God has delivered me from the kingdom and authority of darkness, I do not need any more deliverance. I am already delivered. God said I am delivered and God cannot lie. When I say I do not need to be delivered, I am not making an arrogant statement. I am making a statement of fact based upon the Word of God. How do I speak life to my life? I begin to say, "Praise God, I am free. Praise God, I am delivered from anything that would hold me in bondage — anything, whether it is sex, women, men, cigarettes, whiskey, gambling, lying, fear, or whatever. I have been delivered from all of it."

You might not actually be experiencing that deliverance at a specific point in time, but that is not because you are not delivered. It is only because you do not know any better and you are continuing to accept the bondage. You continue to confess, "Well, I have a problem with sex."

The Word says we can speak either death or life to our life. However, you do not have enough Bible sense to realize you are delivered, and that is why you are having problems. It is because you are confessing it. When you speak the negative you are tying the rope around your own neck by saying, "I have a problem with sex. I have a problem with cigarettes. I have a problem with homosexuality. I have a problem with narcotics or whatever." This is why you have it, because you say you do. God said He set you free from it, but you continue to say you have it. Therefore, you are snared by your words.

If you can ever get this into your spirit where it affects your thinking, when you get ready to pick up that cigarette, you will say, "Wait a minute! What am I doing? I am free! I have been delivered from smoking cigarettes. I do not need this devilish thing. Get away from me in the name of Jesus!" However, if you continue saying you are in bondage, what do you expect a person in bondage to do? He goes right back and wallows in that mud!

You must say, "I am free! This is below my dignity. I have been set free. I cannot indulge in this kind of activity. I used to be in bondage to cocaine. I used to be hung up on sex. I used to be this, that, or the other, but I am free now. Jesus set me free!" I have to speak that to my life. I have to tell myself that every day. I have to say it until I am actually experiencing it. It is my words that release the power of God in my life.

When you walk into a room and flip the switch on the wall, that is not what creates light. That simply releases the electricity to the light bulb for your benefit. The light is actually potentially there all the time, as long as you pay your electric bill. However, you have to flip the switch to activate it. It is there in essence, but not in manifestation. When you flip the switch, you activate it. It becomes manifested at that point.

Well, likewise, God's deliverance is in you, if you are a child of God. It is already there, but you have to activate it. How do you flip the switch? With your words, by saying, "I am free and delivered from all sinful acts. I am no longer in bondage!" Then you will start acting as if you are free.

HOW TO ACT AS IF YOU ARE DELIVERED

How does a person who is free from nicotine act? They do not buy anymore cigarettes. They do not have any reason to go to the cigarette machine, because they are free from cigarettes. Likewise, they no longer have to meet the pusher on the corner because they are not under the influence of narcotics. What do they need a pusher for? They are free from drugs! They do not need to go to the liquor store because they do not drink anymore; they are delivered from alcoholism.

If you come to my house, one thing is conspicuous in its absence: you will not find an ashtray in my house. What does a non-smoker need with an ashtray? Do you understand me? If you have been delivered from cigarettes, you have no need for an ashtray. What do you need a cigarette lighter for? Get rid of all that stuff that promotes the bondage. Because you are not married and you are delivered from sexual activities, then you keep your chastity belt locked, because unmarried people in Christ do not need sex, right? You are free!

Some people in their squeamish, petrified, fearful perception of God will say, "Brother Price, you can't make any demands on God. You don't have any rights with God." Who says so? No, I cannot arbitrarily demand rights. But I am not doing that. All I am doing is demanding the rights that God said I already have, and I am not demanding them from God, because it is not God who is keeping them from me. I am demanding them from the evil one who I have been delivered from. The evil one does not like the fact that I am delivered and he wants to keep me in bondage. He wants to put dark shades over my eyes so that I will not know the truth, and keep me under his foot. However, I have been set tree from the devil and his evil devices!

God said it. I believe it, and that forever settles it. I have deliverance, so I started acting as if I had it. I started acting like a free person would act, and I started talking like a free person. *Free at last, free at last, thank God Almighty, I am free at last!*

From the Curse to the Blessing

Galatians 3:13 says, Christ has redeemed us from the curse. If you are *from* somewhere that means that you are not presently where you are *from*. Because if you were presently where you are *from*, you would be there now; you would not be *from* there. I could rightfully, biblically say, "I am *from* the curse." This is telling you I am not in the curse now, which means that I am no longer where the curse is. I am somewhere else.

The opposite of the curse would be the blessing. Let me prove that from the Word so that we do not get into speculation. Galatians 3:13-14 says:

13   *Christ has redeemed us from the curse of the*
      law, having become a curse for us (for it is written,
      "Cursed is everyone who hangs on a tree"),

14   *that the blessing of Abraham might come upon the*
      Gentiles in Christ Jesus, that we might receive the
      promise of the Spirit through faith.

Christ has redeemed us from the curse so that the blessing can come. You see, the blessing and the curse cannot occupy one's life at the same point in time. You either have the curse or you have the blessing. You cannot have both. You either have dark or you have light. You cannot have both. Dark is the absence of light, and light is the absence of dark. You cannot have light and darkness at the same point in time.

Christ has redeemed us *from* the curse. This is who I am. I am *from* the curse. You thought my name was Fred Price, but my name is really, "From the Curse." Can you see that? That is where I am from. If I am from the curse, then I am somewhere else. Where am I? I am in the blessing.

What is the curse? I need to know what I have been redeemed *from* so that I can know what I have been redeemed *to*.

Deuteronomy 28:15:

> But it shall come to pass, if you do not obey the
> voice of the LORD your God, to observe carefully
> all His commandments and His statutes which I
> command you today, that all these curses will come
> upon you and overtake you:

Observe to do what? Wait a minute! How can they come upon you and overtake you if they are not already in existence? An automobile on the highway cannot overtake me unless that automobile is on the same highway that I am on. The implication is that these curses are already on the same highway that mankind is on. However, whenever I observe to do all that is written in God's Word, I will stay ahead of the curses.

Notice also in the verse, the word *commandments*. What is the first thing you think of when you hear that word? Right away, we think of the Ten Commandments. I submit to you that this word *commandments* is a synonym for God's Word, which is God's will. However, I have news for you; it is not limited to ten! It means anything and everything that God tells you to do in the Bible. The reason it is referred to as *commandments* is because whenever God Almighty speaks to you, it is not a suggestion.

Deuteronomy 28:16-19:

16   *"Cursed shall you be in the city, and cursed shall you be in the country.*

17   *"Cursed shall be your basket and your kneading bowl.*

18   *"Cursed shall be the fruit of your body and the produce of your land, the increase of your cattle and the offspring of your flocks.*

19   *"Cursed shall you be when you come in, and cursed shall you be when you go out."*

These scriptures tell us of all the curses that shall come and overtake you. This implies they are already here. However, consider this example as an illustration: The Travelers Insurance Co. logo is a red umbrella, and around the umbrella, rain is falling. Underneath the umbrella, it is dry. Their point is that if you are covered by their insurance company, you are protected from all the adverse conditions. The rain is representative of automobile accidents, fires, hazards, and so on.

The Word of God is like that umbrella. As long as you stay under it, observe to do all that God says, then you have the protection of the umbrella. The umbrella—God's Word—does not stop the curses from coming, nor does it do away with the curses so that they are no longer existent. What it does is keep the curses from falling on you.

If you keep up the umbrella of God's protection, you can walk right through the storm, and walk out dry. However, if you do not "observe to do," the curses, which are already here, will come upon you. You have no protection. Keep in mind that the way these verses are worded it appears that God is doing the cursing. However, as I explained in the previous chapters, these verses should have

have been rendered, "the Lord will permit them to come upon you."

The curse should not operate in a Christian's life. However, if you permit it, God has to permit the curse to operate in your life. You are in control. The thing that is so awesome and tragic about this is that even if you do not know what His will is, you are going to pay the consequences anyway. This is why God gave you His Word, so you can read for yourself. You do not have to depend on Fred Price or any other minister of the gospel. We ought to be telling you the truth, and I am, but we are not the final word.

The bottom line is God is going to hold you accountable—especially you who live in America—you have no excuse. You can buy a Bible at the drugstore. You can go to a hotel and spend one night in a room and find a Bible in the drawer. You have no excuse in America not to know the will of God. If you really want to know it, you can know it.

Sickness and disease are curses. They are not blessings. God wants you to avoid them, and He tells you exactly how to do it—observe to do the Word. If you *observe to do*, to follow His statutes, then these things cannot come upon you and overtake you. This means it is not God's will for you to have them. You have been redeemed. If you do not know that, you cannot take advantage of God's promises.

It is sad to say, but the organized church world has been playing games, entertaining folk. It is pathetic and I really feel sorry for the ministers. They will have to stand before Jesus Christ and give an account of what they have done with God's people.

It is tragic, but I did not learn about these truths in the churches that I attended over a seventeen-year period. They did not tell me anything about this. They did not tell me that there was a curse. They did not tell me that if I observed to do the Word of God that I could be exonerated from the curse. They did not tell me about the blessing of Abraham. They did not tell me that Christ has redeemed me from the curse of the law.

Jesus told us that if the blind lead the blind, they both end up in the microwave oven, burnt beyond recognition. God said it many years ago through the mouth of the prophet: *My people are destroyed* [or perish] *for lack of knowledge* (Hosea 4:6). Perish how? With this curse. The curse is blind and it attacks everyone. It has no preference for color, gender, age or sexual orientation. However, the good news is that Christ has redeemed us from the curse.

CHAPTER NINE

FACT 1B:
WHAT WE ARE IN CHRIST:
THE BLESSING OF ABRAHAM

We are still discussing what we are in *Christ*. What am I? I am the redeemed. I have a standing with God. I am His purchased, blood-bought, blood-washed son. I am a son of God. I am the redeemed of the Lord and I am saying so. Christ has redeemed me from the curse of the law so that the blessing of Abraham might come upon me. Here is what is so exciting about it: God has forever settled this issue in heaven. God has made it so abundantly clear that you would have to hire someone and pay them overtime to help you misunderstand this.

THE BLESSING OF ABRAHAM

We read what the curse is and we are going to read a description of the blessing. However, before we do I want to make sure you know that the scriptures we read are talking about you. Sometimes people hear things and they think they cannot relate to it. They cannot believe that this could mean them. You need to know that God is talking about you.

Galatians 3:14:

> *that the blessing of Abraham might come upon the Gentiles in Christ Jesus, that we might receive the promise of the Spirit through faith.*

Abraham lived before the Old Testament or Old Covenant was instituted. However, Abraham's historical account is contained in the context of the Old Covenant.

Galatians 3:7:

> *Therefore know that only those who are of faith are sons of Abraham.*

Abraham is called the father of the faithful. What does that mean? This is letting us know we have a spiritual relationship with Abraham, in that Abraham was a man of faith. He believed God, as stated in the Bible. Jesus Christ did not come to the earth during the time that Abraham lived. Jesus did not die at Calvary during the time Abraham lived. Jesus did not rise from the dead or ascend to the right hand of the Father during the time Abraham lived. As a result, Abraham could never accept Jesus Christ as his personal Savior and Lord. He never had that opportunity.

If Abraham could not accept Jesus Christ as his personal Savior and Lord that would mean that Abraham could never be born again. Abraham could not be born again, that would mean that

Abraham could not be saved. In short, Abraham was not a Christian and could not participate in anything spiritual because he would be dead in trespasses and sin. In other words, he was spiritually dead.

If God blessed Abraham before Jesus came to this world, it means that there is only one way that God could have blessed Abraham, and that would have to be with material things because he was not spiritually alive. He could not relate to God spiritually because Christ had not come yet.

The Bible says in Acts 4:12:

> *Nor is there salvation in any other, for there is no other name under heaven given among men by which we must be saved.*

This name was not given to Abraham, so how could he be saved? He could not. If he was not saved, then he was a sinner. Just like anybody who lives today who has not yet accepted Christ. Abraham was a sinner and God had to deal with Abraham as a sinner, as a physical man, not as a spiritual man.

When the Bible says *that the blessing of Abraham might come upon the Gentiles,* then the blessing must be a physical blessing. We get our spiritual blessing from where? From Jesus. Because Jesus has come, Jesus has died, Jesus has risen, Jesus has ascended and we have accepted Him. Therefore, our spiritual relationship with God comes as a result of our connection with Jesus. Our physical relationship with God comes as the result of our connection with Abraham, our faithful father.

Consider Galatians 3:9:

> *So then those who are of faith are blessed with believing Abraham.*

When it says we who are of faith are the children of Abraham, it means that like Abraham believed God and God gave him credit for being righteous, as we believe God by faith, we are declared righteous. In that sense, they that are of faith are the children of Abraham.

When you find out how Abraham was blessed, you will understand why the material aspect of the gospel is so often criticized. The purpose of the criticism is to frighten you off and intimidate you from ever receiving this blessing. Satan knows that if you ever become financially and materially independent of the circumstances, you will then have at your fingertips, the resources to promote the gospel like it ought to be promoted, without any hindrances. He knows if that happens, there will be an onslaught made against the gates of his kingdom, and those gates will not be able to stand against the onslaught of the Word of God. You see, it costs big money to promote the gospel.

The curse and blessing are revealed in Deuteronomy 28. Verses 1-3 God, speaking through the mouth of the prophet, says:

1   *"Now it shall come to pass, if you diligently obey the voice of the LORD your God, to observe carefully all His commandments which I command you today, that the LORD your God will set you high above all nations of the earth.*

2   *"And all these blessings shall come upon you and overtake you, because you obey the voice of the LORD your God:*

3   *"Blessed shall you be in the city, and blessed shall you be in the country."*

You do not have to move to the suburbs to be blessed. People have been migrating from the inner cities of our nation into the seclusion and, in their minds, the safety of the suburbs. Some people believe God can only operate outside the city limits. They believe God is handicapped if you stay in the inner city and that He can only work in the suburbs.

He said, *Blessed shall you be in the city* . . . . I am not leaving the city. You can spend 65-90 minutes going one way trying to get away from the city. You can drive to the suburbs and beat your brains out on the freeways every day if you want to, smelling all that exhaust smoke for 90 minutes or more.

Some of you were born in the suburbs. To you, that was life. You do not have to leave the suburbs or the fields to come into the city to be blessed. You can be blessed where you are, if you hearken to the voice of the Lord your God. You can be blessed in the suburbs, and I can be blessed in the city, close to my home and my job. I do not have to get on a freeway to get to my home or to my job. Amen! Hallelujah! Eat your heart out, you daily freeway drivers.

Deuteronomy 28:4:

> *Blessed shall be the fruit of your body* [This is talking about childbearing. Your seed will be blessed and this is good news. You can expect to have a healthy baby if you know how to use your faith.], *the produce of your ground* [notice He said your ground] *and the increase of your herds, the increase of your cattle and the offspring of your flocks.*

God is saying everything you are involved with ought to be blessed. My ground is my ministry which God entrusted to me. This is the soil, the ground that I have to work and plant in. I do not care what somebody else's ground is doing. I do not have to listen to those who might say, "This is all you can do here in this part of the city because this is a blighted area, this is the ghetto." Yes, but did you know that both garden and ghetto begin with a "g." You can turn the ghetto into a garden, a Garden of Eden if you have the faith to believe it.

It is up to you whether your ground is blessed or not. As for me and my house, I am expecting a big harvest. A gigantic, brontosaurus-sized harvest! Because I am planting good seed in that ground, and my Father God told me, "Blessed shall be the fruit of my ground." This is my ministry to grow. I expect my ministry to produce results in the lives of others, because that is the seed I am planting, the Word of God, and your lives are the soil in which that seed is planted. I am expecting results. I am suppose to have everything I want to have and everything I can believe God for. I have it recorded in my Father's Word.

There is a spiritual law of sowing and reaping—thank God that no man can abrogate it. If you plant good seed into good ground, you will get a harvest, and nobody can stop it. The classroom may be your ground. Or the filling station may be your ground. Wherever you are, that is your ground and you ought to expect it to be blessed if you are doing all the things that the voice of the Lord has called you to do and everything you know to do.

Deuteronomy 28:5:

> *Blessed shall be your basket and your*
> *kneading bowl.*

The basket and bowl represent what was brought and stored up until it was needed, because they did not use everything right away. When I was a little boy, my parents used to store preserves. Throughout the winter, we would eat good vegetables and fruits from those jars of preserves, or canned goods. In this day and age, perhaps your basket and bowl is your bank account or your investments. If you are spending everything you get and have nothing left over, then you are not blessed yet.

Deuteronomy 28:6:

> *Blessed shall you be when you come in,*
> *and blessed shall you be when you go out.*

In other words, a blessing should be waiting for you when you leave home and go out into the street. Are you getting the message that God wants you blessed? I love it! Many of you are missing out on it because you are not looking for the blessing. Do you look for it? We often pass right over things that are blessings, because we are looking for some great big atomic explosion. God does not always speak in the thunder. Sometimes it is the still small voice. You have to be sensitive and open so that you do not miss out on your blessings. Sometimes things can seem so inconsequential that you miss it and take it for granted, yet it could be the blessing of our life. I expect to be blessed when I go out and blessed when I come in. God told me I am blessed and not cursed.

Deuteronomy 28:7-8:

> 7   *"The LORD will cause your enemies who rise*
> *against you to be defeated before your face; they*
> *shall come out against you one way and flee*
> *before you seven ways.*

> 8   *"The LORD will command the blessing on you in*
> *your storehouses and in all to which you set your*
> *hand, and He will bless you in the land which the*
> *LORD your God is giving you."*

At the time this was enunciated, it was spoken from a historical point of view, to Israel when they were about to go into the land that God had promised them. However, ultimately, this truth was for all of God's people from generation to generation.

God has given us a land. We have been translated out of darkness into the kingdom of God's dear Son. Our land is the land of walking in the realm of the Spirit. Our land flows with milk and honey, and we are supposed to be blessed and victorious in that land. We are supposed to enjoy a life of abundance!

God said my storehouses will be blessed. My storehouse would be wherever I am storing up something. Like my bank account and investment portfolio. This means I should make the highest rate of interest available, compounded daily. I ought to be blessed so that I can be a blessing. Everything you set your hand to, God will command the blessing upon it. This is why I believe my ministry is blessed and always will be blessed.

Psalm 1:1-3:

1   *Blessed is the man who walks not in the counsel of the ungodly, nor stands in the path of sinners, nor sits in the seat of the scornful;*

2   *But his delight is in the law of the LORD, and in His law he meditates day and night.*

3   *He shall be like a tree planted by the rivers of water, that brings forth its fruit in its season, whose leaf also shall not wither; and whatever he does shall prosper.*

This sounds exactly like . . . *blessed in all that you set your hand to.* God said whatsoever you do, it shall prosper. It is for this reason, I confess, "I am blessed going out and I am blessed coming in. I am blessed in all that I do." When I say that, I am speaking life to my life and that creates the reality of it in my life.

Deuteronomy 28:9-11:

9   *"The LORD will establish you as a holy people to Himself, just as He has sworn to you, if you keep the commandments of the LORD your God and walk in His ways.*

10   *"Then all peoples of the earth shall see that you are called by the name of the LORD, and they shall be afraid of you.*

11   *"And the LORD will grant you plenty of goods, in the fruit of your body, in the increase of your livestock, and in the produce of your ground, in the land of which the LORD swore to your fathers to give you."*

The people of Israel spent their labor in the field, with the cattle, living off the land. They were an agrarian society. Whatever your area of endeavor is where you spend your labor. God said you will have plenty of goods—predicated, of course, on your diligent obedience to the voice of the Lord your God and to do His Word. If you are not listening, seeing, and doing, then these blessings will not be manifested in your life.

Remember, the land that the Lord has given us is the kingdom of God when we were born again. We still live in the world, we are physical creatures, but we are not limited to and should not be governed by the world system.

Deuteronomy 28:12:

The LORD will open to you His good treasure, the heavens, to give the rain to your land in its season, and to bless all the work of your hand. You shall lend to many nations, but you shall not borrow.

How can the Lord open to you His good treasure? Simple, because He has no bad treasure. God is good, so His treasure would have to be good. Jesus made reference to this truth when He said; You cannot get sweet water out of a bitter fountain. You do not get grapes off of a bramble bush. Everything produces after its kind.

James 1:17 is a New Testament scripture that corroborates what I have said:

> *Every good gift and every perfect gift is from above,*
> *and comes down from the Father of lights, with*
> *whom there is no variation or shadow of turning.*

If every good gift and every perfect gift is from above, then every bad gift and every imperfect gift is from beneath, or from hell. Whatever is hellish in nature comes from Satan. Whatever is good in nature comes from heaven. Because there is no variableness in God, He does not change. He is consistent. He cannot be good one day and bad the next. If His good ever becomes bad, then it is variable, it has changed and that would invalidate His Word. This is good news!

Let me ask you a very pointed question: Have you diligently obeyed the voice of the Lord? Have you observed His Word? Are you doing His Word? If your answer is "yes" then say these words: "All the work of my hand is prospering and will continue to prosper because I have diligently obeyed the voice of the Lord and I have observed to do all of His commandments."

Deuteronomy 28:11-12 tell us that "*. . . the LORD will grant you plenty of goods . . . . You shall lend to many nations, but you shall not borrow.*"

This lets us know that we will be able to lend and not have to borrow because we will have plenty.

There are many Christians in this so-called "faith walk" who believe that you should not borrow anything from a lending institution, and they cite Deuteronomy 28:12 as a proof text.

However, this verse does not say it is wrong to borrow. It simply says you will have so much surplus, that you will not have a need to borrow. It is obvious that borrowing could not be wrong because, if so, then lending would have to be wrong, since it is lending that causes borrowing.

I think that the Body of Christ should be the nation that does the lending—not necessarily to the nations of the world, but to the nations of the Body of Christ. You could think of a state as a nation or you could think of a group of people as a nation, or you could think of a local church as a nation that may need money. We could lend to them, but we cannot if we do not have it.

Deuteronomy 28:13:

> And the LORD will make you the head and not the tail; you shall be above only, and not be beneath, if you heed the commandments of the LORD your God, which I command you today, and are careful to observe them.

Do you like that? The head and not the tail, because when you are the tail, you get wagged by somebody else. Tails do not wag dogs; dogs wag tails. If we are the tail, we get wagged, and, in this case, by Satan.

What are we in Christ? We are the blessed. We are the plenteous in goods. We are the head; we are not the tail. You need to see yourself that way. No matter what circumstances may present to your view, you must look at the circumstances and point the finger of the Word of God at them and tell them, "I am the blessed of the Lord. I am not the cursed!"

At first you may not see any change in those circumstances when you begin to say that, but you must be consistent. It is like a farmer. You cannot plant a seed on Monday and expect a harvest on Tuesday. Then because you don't see the results on Tuesday, you dig up the field. You will never get a harvest that way. The farmer has to believe the seed is working, that the seed he planted is alive. And, because he believes it is alive he waters it on a daily basis. If he sees weeds coming up, he plucks the weeds up so they do not choke the seed.

The farmer has not seen a thing, yet it is amazing the faith that he has in the seed. He is watering it. This what we have to do with our words. We plant the seed of God's Word in our lives by speaking His Word. My confession must be in line with God's Words, such as: "Praise God, I believe I am healed. Thank you, Father, I believe I am healed." What am I doing? I am watering my seed of faith with God's Word.

When I first prayed, I said, 'With Jesus stripes I was healed," I planted the seed. Then every day after that, until I see the harvest, the manifestation in my physical body, I water the seed: "Father, thank You, I believe I am healed. I believe I am healed." Then one day, when the plant comes up, when the condition disappears, I can say, "Praise God, I am healed!" You have to have faith and tenacity to stay with your confession of faith—just like the farmer does.

A long time passes before the farmer actually sees any results of his planting, but he has already made preparations for where he will store his crops. He is preparing the trucks and the reaping machines. Why? Because he is expecting a crop to come out of that ground. He planted good seed in good ground and there is something built into the seed that will produce a harvest. He has done his part and he is expecting. You ought to expect a harvest in Christ Jesus. Glory be to God!

The exciting thing about this crop—if you ever learn to plant right and water right—is that planting of the Word into your life by the confession of your mouth will produce a daily harvest and not a seasonal one. Once you get the seed in the ground, keep it there, water it, feed it, and stay with it. Once it starts producing, it produces a crop every day. This is the exciting part about it.

My philosophy is this: You might as well plant, because time is going to pass anyway, even if you do not do anything. You could not be any worse off, so you cannot do anything but win.

Deuteronomy 28:14:

> *So you shall not turn aside from any of the words*
> *which I command you this day, to the right or the*
> *left, to go after other gods to serve them.*

God commands you to do His Word—*commandments* and the *Word of God* mean the same thing. God's words are commands, they are never suggestions. Do not get hung up on the so-called Ten Commandments because God told us more than ten things to do!

YOU ARE AN HEIR OF GOD!

Galatians 4:6-7:

> 6   *And because you are sons, God has sent forth the*
>   *Spirit of His Son into your hearts, crying out,*
>   *"Abba, Father!"*

> 7   *Therefore you are no longer a slave but a son,*
>   *and if a son, then an heir of God through Christ.*

How much does God have? Everything! Well, you are an heir of God through Christ, so you should have everything you need and then some. Stop belittling yourself. Stop listening to the lie of the enemy through the system, telling you how inferior you are, how homely you are, how ugly you are, how pretty you are, how handsome you are. You do not need man to tell you who you are. Let God tell you who you are.

Your feet are too big. God did not say they were too big. Your nose is too big. God never said these negative things about you. Therefore, do not let people tell you that junk. You tell them your nose is perfect, functional and does everything God ordained it to do. I am a son of God. I am not a slave of God. I am a son, and because I am a son, I am an heir of God. I love it! Think about it: Jesus already died, so the inheritance is now! Our inheritance is not waiting for us in heaven. The inheritance is in this life now!

Understand you are not a son of God just because you go to church. You are not a son of God just because you came up in what is called, "a Christian home." You are only a son of God if you have personally and individually—by an act of your will—accepted and confessed Him as the Lord of your life. This is what marked you a son of God.

CHAPTER TEN

FACT 2:

WHERE WE ARE IN CHRIST

The second thing we must learn to confess in order to live the victorious Christian life is *where we are in Christ.* This refers to our position or our standing with Christ. You have probably heard people say, "How do you stand with so-and-so?" However, the more important question is: "How do you stand with God?"

It is easy to flippantly say, "I am a son of God." This is great and true, but what does it really mean in terms of the everyday life that we have to live? What is my real position? Or, do I have a position? What is my standing? Or is it just, "I am going to miss hell when I die and go to heaven?

heaven." Is this it? The rest of the time, we just struggle through and make it the best way we can?

Unfortunately, that is the mentality of the average Christian. It was my mentality for years. The churches that I attended did not tell me any better. They just said, "Hold on. Hang in there. Keep a stiff upper lip. Keep sending up timber every day; trying to get ready to put on that long white robe." This was all they gave me, as far as how to deal with life.

However, the good news is that we do have a position, a standing in Christ, and we need to know what it is. Many Christians are living a life of oppression, defeat, and fear at the hand of Satan, simply because they do not know their position in Christ. They do not know how they really stand with God. You should be just as sure about where you stand with God and Christ as you are about your own name. Most Christians believe they have been crucified with Christ, because they have heard that all their Christian life, and this is true. Nonetheless, we need to understand and then operate in our position of power and authority here on earth.

Paul says in Galatians 2:20:

> *I have been crucified with Christ; it is no longer I who live, but Christ lives in me; and the life which I now live in the flesh I live by faith in the Son of God, who loved me and gave Himself for me.*

Paul says, "I am crucified with Christ." This is a statement of "identification," and it belongs to every child of God. God sees us identified with Christ. When Jesus died at Calvary, Fred Price died at Calvary. When Jesus went into the grave, Fred Price went into the grave. When Jesus rose from the dead after three days and three nights, Fred Price rose from the dead. This is how God sees me, and I have to learn to see me the same way.

Second Corinthians 5:14:

> *For the love of Christ compels us, because we judge thus: that if One died for all, then all died;*

Many Christians are aware that Christ has died for them, but don't understand how this act of love affects their position. Others have dared to believe they have risen with Christ, according to Colossians 3:1. *If then you were raised with Christ, seek those things which are above, where Christ is, sitting at the right hand of God. This again is identification.* We have risen with Christ. However, this still does not tell me my present-day position with Christ. Even though the Word of God tells us that we have been crucified, died, and risen, multitudes of Christians are still living a defeated life, and that is where the rubber meets the road. If all you believe is not affecting your daily existence, then what good is it?

When you talk about going to heaven and all that comes with it, you are talking about something that is abstract and nebulous. The only conscious life you really know is this one. I believe in heaven, and by faith I take what the Bible says about it, but I have never experienced it yet. We have to understand that not only were we crucified with Christ, not only did we die with Christ, not only did we rise with Christ, but the most important thing is that we *ascended* with Him.

Ephesians 1:19-21:

> 19   *and what is the exceeding greatness of His power toward us* [Underline the words, *greatness of His power toward us.* If you are a believer, then His power has been committed to you.] *who believe, according to the working of His mighty power*

20   *which He worked in Christ when He raised Him from the dead and seated Him at His right hand in the heavenly places,*

21   *far above all principality and power* [This word *power* means "authority."] *and might and dominion, and every name that is named, not only in this age but also in that which is to come.*

When God says this about Jesus, He is talking about Fred; He is talking about you. As you read verse 21 over and over, you will begin to see and appreciate the enormity of this great privilege that we have.

The word *principality* in that verse refers to angelic beings of all ranks—angels, archangels, seraphim, cherubim; no matter who they are, we are above them in Christ Jesus. As mentioned above, the word *power* is the Greek word for "authority." We are above all authority, except of course, God Himself. We are above the authority that Satan has in this earth realm. We are above all the might, which means "strength," of Satan, demons, or anyone else. Dominion means "rulership," or "control." If you can get a picture of that in your heart, you will kick the devil in his backside and get him out of your business.

If any business on this plant and in this society should succeed, it ought to be your business—providing you know what you are doing. If you do not know all you need to know, ask God for wisdom. The Bible says that Christ has given us wisdom. Therefore, you ought to succeed.

Paul says, *far above . . . every name that is named.* Is *fear* a name? Then we are above fear. Is *poverty* a name? Then we are above poverty. Is *welfare* a name? Then we are above welfare. Is *cancer* a name? Then we are far above cancer. Is *sickness* a name? Is *disease* a name? We are far above all that is satanic and you should not tolerate sickness or disease in your body.

Yes, it will try to come against you. However, you should stand in front of it and say, "Wait a minute! I have ascended with Christ!" How much sickness affects Jesus? None. If you are seated together in heavenly places in Christ, then it should not affect you either. Satan—the enemy, who brings the sickness and disease to you, will try to intimidate you by putting thoughts in your mind and getting you to confess them and own them as yours. Death and life are in the power of the tongue. You can control the circumstances of life with your words.

I believe there is a place in God where we can walk above the circumstances. He says far above every name that is named. In other words, we win all the time!

Ephesians 2:5:

> *even when we were dead in trespasses, made us alive together with Christ (by grace you have been saved),*

Therefore, when Jesus was made alive, we were made alive with Him. God saw us made alive through Jesus. When Christ was raised, Fred was raised. Do you see the importance of that statement? Are you going to accept defeat? Are you going to let the circumstances whip your head? Are you going to let the system tell you what you can achieve in this life? No way! Read that scripture again: It says, "raised you up together, and made you sit together in the welfare office." Well, read it again: "raised you up together, and made you sit together in the junk yard; in the Goodwill store; in that place where they sell day old bread."

This is the mentality that many Christians have. They let the system dictate to them and say, "That is all—you should not have or want any more than that." However, this is not so, because you have been raised together with Christ. You are seated together with Him in heavenly places. You have ascended with Jesus and you are entitled to what He has and paid for with His life and blood.

HOW DO YOU DEFEAT THE ENEMY?

Think about this: God has not called us to contend with Satan for a place of victory, we are already victorious in Christ. I am not going into the squared circle and put the gloves on to find out who is champion. I am going into the squared circle because I am the champion! Knowing that you are a champion already makes a big difference. Your whole attitude is different. We already have the victory. We do not have to go somewhere and get it. We have it now, but we will never experience it unless we begin to confess, see and act victorious.

You have to get a new vision of who you are in Christ. I am a winner. I am a victor. I am a champion. I am on top. I am the head, not the tail. This principle does not only work in the area of "things," it works in every area, even husband-wife relationships. You ought to have a tranquil, peaceful, blessed, loving, sexually fulfilling, emotionally fulfilling, and spiritually fulfilling relationship with your spouse. Each morning you wake up it should not be, "Oh no! She's up again! Let me get away from this woman!" Unfortunately, this is the way many Christian couples act.

The Church world as a whole has not done what Jesus said, which is, "Feed my sheep and feed my lambs." Churches, for the most part, have been entertaining people. This is particularly true in black churches. I have to say that, because I have not been privileged to worship in the Hispanic, Asian, or Caucasian churches over a protracted period of time. However, I have been in black churches for years, and I am telling you it is pathetic. The worship service is mostly emotional entertainment, geared to stimulating an emotional feeling, rather than imparting information. The churches should give you the wisdom of God, show you who you are, what you have, and what you can do, not just give you a "feeling."

Too many churches present either emotionalism or on the other extreme, intellectualism. In those settings, it is so quiet you can hear a pin drop on carpet, and still you have not learned anything that can sustain your spirit man. You hear such things as, "God is mind. God is the great universal spirit." Big deal! How does that help you pay the bills? How does that destroy that 105-degree temperature in your child before brain damage occurs?

Let us find out how we can be victorious over Satan, beginning with Luke 10:17:

> *Then the seventy returned with joy, saying,*
> *"Lord, even the demons are subject to us in*
> *Your name."*

This is an absolutely astounding revelation. Jesus has commissioned these men to (1) go out at His behest and do some work for Him; (2) go ahead of Him into the cities that He would later go to Himself. He gave them a special dispensation of authority and told them to heal the sick, raise the dead, cast out demons, freely you have received, freely give. And, they went out. The disciples were not born-again or Spirit-filled Christians at that time. They were just followers of Jesus, yet they came back with joy.

I wonder how much authority we, those of us who are blood-bought, blood-washed, and Spirit-filled have over the demons? We, the sons of God, whose names are written in the Lamb's Book of Life, who have the sword of the Spirit, the written Word of God ought to be operating in joy everyday, instead of sadness and heaviness.

Luke 10:18-19:

18   *And He said to them, "I saw Satan fall like*
      lightning from heaven.

19   *"Behold, I give you the authority to trample on*
      serpents and scorpions, and over all the power of
      the enemy, and nothing shall by any means hurt
      you."

141

This is how you can defeat the enemy. This is how you can go into the squared circle as a champion and defeat any opponent that comes against you. You have been delegated authority by Jesus Christ, the Head of the Church!

Look at verse 19 again. I think it is awesome when He says; nothing shall by any means hurt you. There is not a means in existence that can hurt you! I can tell you exactly what happened in a lot of your minds as you read those words. Experiences returned to your mind, and you began remembering people you believe were real good Christians. You began to think of your own life, and how many times you have been hurt.

But wait a minute! How long have you been confessing that you have risen with Christ? Or that you have ascended with Him? Or that you are seated at the right hand of the Father? How long have you been speaking words of life to your life, instead of words of death? How long have you been saying with your mouth that you are a champion? If you are honest, you have not been confessing these truths. As a result, you have been hurt. You did not know these truths and you cannot take advantage of what you do not know.

The devil does not play fair. He does not care that you do not know your rights in Christ. In fact, he likes it better when you do not know.

I am here to tell you that if what we have read is not true, then Jesus lied to us. However, thank God, He did not lie! He said, Behold, I give to you authority [which also means "right" or "privilege"]. Therefore, Jesus is telling us. "Behold, I give to you authority, right or privilege over all the enemy's ability." I like it!

It does not matter how big your ability is. When you are the one in authority, ability is irrelevant and immaterial. If you have a military general who is just 4 feet 5 inches tall, he has the authority to command the guy who is 6 feet 7 inches tall. It is not about your size. Do not look at yourself in your own eyes. Look at yourself through the eyes of God. You are a giant.

Confess Luke 10:19 daily. You need to say it out loud, not necessarily to your friends or relations, because they will think you have gone stark raving mad. You can say it out loud while you are driving in your car, when you are behind closed doors, in your garage, in the pantry. You need to say it out loud so that your own ears can hear it. Faith comes by hearing, and hearing, and hearing, and hearing, and hearing, and hearing.

Keep telling yourself you are a giant, based on the Word of God. I am not talking about a psych job; I am talking about what God said about us. God cannot lie, so that means this is who I am —a spiritual giant. If you keep saying it, confessing it, you will finally get to the point where you will begin to believe "that you are somebody." When you do this you will become bold in the things of God instead of timid and easily intimidated. You will become the intimidator to Satan and the demons. When morning comes and the alarm clock rings, all the demons in hell will say, "Oh, no! Fred's up again! Look out, the giant is up again!"

After Jesus was resurrected, but prior to going back to heaven to sit down at the right hand of the Majesty on High, Jesus said in Matthew 28:18:

> And Jesus came and spoke to them, saying,
> "All authority [all right or privilege]
> has been given to Me in heaven and on
> earth.

I have shown you two scriptures that say all authority is given to me. How much of the authority? All of it. This leaves nothing out. What do you suppose that all power in heaven and in earth was given to Him for? To use it! Can you agree with that?

Matthew 28:19-20:

> 19   "Go therefore [Jesus says this based on what
>   He said in verse 18—that all authority has
>   been given to man.) and make disciples of all

> *the nations, baptizing them in the name of*
> *the Father and of the Son and of the Holy*
> *Spirit,*
>
> 20   *"teaching them to observe all things that*
> *I have commanded you; and lo, I am with*
> *you always, even to the end of the age." Amen.*

After Jesus made this statement, what happened? He left. Where did He leave to go? He went back to heaven. It has been more than 1,900 years ago. Now tell me how much time has Jesus Christ spent on this planet since then? None. Where has Jesus been? At the right hand of the Father interceding on behalf of the believers.

Jesus said, *"All authority* [all right or privilege) *has been given to Me in heaven and on earth."* He has not been here on the earth. What good does the authority do Him? He has not been here, but when He left here and went back to heaven, He left His Body, the Church. Jesus empowered the Church to exercise His authority here in this earth realm, while He exercises the authority in the heavenly realm. He delegated all the power to the Church.

If we have all the power, what are we doing defeated? What are we doing sick, whipped and beat down? Why are we going with our needs unmet when we have all the power, all the authority? It does not make sense. It is because we have not understood where we are in Christ. We have not understood our position in Christ.

The ball is in our court. Whatever we bind on earth is bound in heaven; whatever we loose on earth is loosed in heaven. The opposite is also true, whatever we do not bind on earth will not be bound in heaven, and whatever we do not loose on earth will not be loosed in heaven.

My little finger has as much authority as my nose. My nose has as much authority as my foot, because my foot is as much

Fred Price as my head is. Well, we are the Body of Christ. The head is no more Jesus than the feet are. Jesus is Jesus, the head is Jesus, but so is the Body—us Christians.

We do not have to go somewhere and contend with Satan for a place of victory. We already have it because it has been given to us. Jesus delegated the authority to us in this earth realm by the power of attorney, ratified by the High Court in heaven. We have the right to use His name to transact business in His absence and the High Court will recognize it. When I sign the name of Jesus, the High Court of heaven will back it up, and every demon in hell understands and bows his knee, because I am a channel of God. This is where we are. This is our position in Jesus. We are victors because all of Christ's victory is our victory.

You have all the authority contained in God's Word. Nevertheless, we have to take our authority by force, because we have an enemy, Satan. He is our opposition, and that opposition does not want us to operate in our authority. Satan wants to contain us, quarantine us, and render us inoperative.

GOD WILL NOT HONOR MEANINGLESS RITUALISM

Amos 5:21-22:

21   *"I hate, I despise your feast days, and I do not savor your sacred assemblies.*

22   *Though you offer Me burnt offerings and your grain offerings, I will not accept them, nor will I regard your fattened peace offerings.*

145

The thing that is so tragic is that, traditionally, the Church has played right into the hands of the enemy. Religions have bogged the people down in traditions, in ritualistic precepts, rather than the Word of the living God and God will not honor ritualism. God will not honor religious traditions. I am sorry, He will not do it. We have no scripture to support religion.

However, I do have scripture to support what Jesus said in Matthew 28, *"All authority has been given to Me in heaven and on earth."* Then in Mark 16:17 Jesus said, *"And these signs will follow those who believe: In My name"* — this is delegated authority. *In My name . . . .* Understand, we do not do it in our name. We do it in the name of Jesus, and He ratifies it. He says "Yes and Amen" to it, because He is not here on earth physically, but we are, we are His Body. Therefore, what we do, He do(es). It is the same as though He were here on earth doing it Himself. This is how God sees it.

To my understanding, the strongest affirmative statement that you can make in English is, "I will" do thus and so. Jesus said, *"And these signs will follow those who believe."* It does not say that the signs *may* follow. Right away, you are alerted to the fact that if these signs do not follow — whatever those signs are — then it means we are not *believing.* If the signs are not following me, and I say I believe, then either I am a liar or Jesus is a liar.

What are the signs that follow them that believe? According to Mark 16:17: (1) *In My name they will cast out demons.* You cannot cast out a demon if you do not believe there are such things as demons. Many in the Church world do not believe in evil spirits, but Jesus believes in evil spirits. Do you think you are smarter than Jesus? This scripture goes on to say, (2) they will speak with new tongues.... The word *tongue is* the Greek word *glossa,* or *glosse.* The English word *glossolalia,* comes from the Greek and it refers to languages. It is not talking about a sinner who used to use profanity cleaning up his language and now uses nice words. This word refers to speaking with other languages than those that you have learned. It is talking about the same thing that the Apostle Paul talked about in 1 Corinthians 12, 13, and 14. It is the same word talked about in Acts 8, 10, and 19. My friend that is the Bible.

You say you believe?

"Oh, yes, hallelujah, I believe."

Jesus said, These signs will follow those who believe. You say you believe, but you do not speak with other tongues. Either you are lying or Jesus lied. Now, who can you believe and trust in?

Notice that the latter part of that 17th verse said, "they will." It did not say, "they might;" it did not say, "some will and some will not." The verse says they that believe will speak.

"We do not believe in speaking with tongues."

If you do not believe in speaking with tongues, you do not believe in the Bible. Mark 16:17 are the words of Jesus Christ, not Fred Price.

Mark 16:18:

> "They will take up serpents; and if they drink
> anything deadly, it will by no means hurt them;
> they will lay hands on the sick, and they will
> recover."

This is not talking about going up into the Ozarks somewhere, playing with rattlesnakes to prove whether you have faith or not. This is talking about being accidentally bitten by a viper. We have a biblical account of this, when on the Island of Melita, Paul picked up that bundle of sticks and a viper grabbed his hand. Paul shook it off in the fire and it did not bother him in the least.

Do they lay hands on the sick in your church? If they do not, your church does not believe. The only thing that would exonerate you and your church from laying hands on the sick would be that there are no sick people in your congregation.

147

Unfortunately, there is no shortage of sick people in the churches. If God wants the believers to lay hands on the sick, then it is obvious that He does not want the healthy to be sick. This proves that divine healing is for us today. If God's will is for us to be sick, He would not have offered a way out of sickness.

During all the years I was in the Baptist church, they never prayed for the sick. They never preached any sermons, or taught on healing. The only thing I ever heard relative to sickness, disease, and healing was that Christians do not get healed anymore. I was told that all the healings ceased when the last apostle died. The sad thing about it was the church was full of sick people and I was one of them.

To further illustrate the principle of where we are in Christ or, our position in Christ, let us look at the story referred to as the prodigal son in Luke 15:11-31:

11 *Then He said: "A certain man had two sons.*

12 *"And the younger of them said to his father, 'Father, give me the portion of goods that falls to me.' So he divided to them his livelihood.*

13 *"And not many days after, the younger son gathered all together, journeyed to a far country, and there wasted his possessions with prodigal living.*

14 *"But when he had spent all, there arose a severe famine in that land, and he began to be in want.*

15 *"Then he went and joined himself to a citizen of that country, and he sent him into his fields to feed swine.*

16 *"And he would gladly have filled his stomach with the pods that the swine ate, and no one gave him anything.*

17 *"But when he came to himself, he said, 'How many of my father's hired servants have bread enough and to spare, and I perish with hunger!*

18 *'I will arise and go to my father, and will say to him, "Father, I have sinned against heaven and before you,*

19 *"and I am no longer worthy to be called your son. Make me like one of your hired servants."*

20 *"And he arose and came to his father. But when he was still a great way off, his father saw him and had compassion, and ran and fell on his neck and kissed him.*

21 *"And the son said to him, 'Father, I have sinned against heaven and in your sight, and am no longer worthy to be called your son.'*

22 *"But the father said to his servants, 'Bring out the best robe and put it on him, and put a ring on his hand and sandals on his feet.*

23 *'And bring the fatted calf here and kill it, and let us eat and be merry;*

24 *'for this my son was dead and is alive again; he was lost and is found.' And they began to be merry.*

25 *"Now his older son was in the field. And as he came and drew near to the house, he heard music and dancing.*

26 *"So he called one of the servants and asked what these things meant.*

27 *"And he said to him, 'Your brother has come, and because he has received him safe and sound, your father has killed the fatted calf.'*

28 *"But he was angry* [Now there are some Christians who get angry with the Fred Prices of the ministry, because we live and talk about prosperity, victory, and faith.] *and would not go in. Therefore his father came out and pleaded with him.*

29 *"So he answered and said to his father, 'Lo, these many years I have been serving you; I never transgressed your commandment at any time; and yet you never gave me a young goat, that I might make merry with my friends.*

30 *'But as soon as this son of yours came, who has devoured your livelihood with harlots, you killed the fatted calf for him.'*

I call your attention to the next few words. God forbid that they should be words which apply to you.

31   *"And he said to him* [the father said to the elder
       son), *'Son, you are always with me, and all that I
       have is yours.'"*

Similarly, it does not matter that one boy's name was Baptist, and one boy's name was Presbyterian. These names do not make any difference to God. All that have confessed Jesus as their Savior and Lord are in the same family of God. Verse 31 is saying, "Son, you are always with me, but you never asked me for what is yours. You never acknowledged that you needed help."

Too many Christians are like the elder son. Instead of asking, they have been going around as spokesmen for God, telling people what God will not do and they have nothing with which to back it up scripturally. This is what religion has done and continues to do today. God's Word says that the Lord is good and His mercy endures forever. He has not changed even though the last biblical apostle has died.

The scripture says that the father ran out and met the boy before the boy ever arrived at the house. The awesome fact is, the father could not go out and meet the son unless the son was on his way back. In the same manner, God cannot come out and meet you unless you are willing to come back. Come back from religion, traditions, and ritualism.

"Son, you are always with me, and all that I have is yours." Just ask. Many Christians are like that angry son. They are sitting in the midst of plenty, yet they are starving to death. They need to do like the younger son who finally realized, "Here I am starving to death and my father's servants have more to eat than I have. I will arise and go to my father and tell him I messed up. I blew it. I sinned. I failed. I do not ask you to take me back as your son, just take me back as one of your hired servants, and I will be happy with that. It is better than what I have had in that pigpen." In spite of the boy's transgressions, the father was waiting for him to return.

You have a position in Jesus and do not know it. You are a winner and do not know it. You are the head and not the tail, and do not know it, and you do not have enough biblical sense to find out about it. The father told his older son, you are always with me, and all that I have is yours. This is what the heavenly Father is telling us.

Remember, victory will never be yours until you begin to confess that it is yours. Say this out loud: "Victory will never be mine until I begin to confess it as mine!" However, there are guidelines that must be observed in order for you to get it. For instance, the boy had to come out of the pigpen. Many of you are still in the pigpens of life. You have to come out of the pigpen. You cannot be victorious if you are going to live in the pigpens of life!

You have to get your mind renewed with the Word of God. You may have to separate yourself from some people you have been associating with. You may have to leave some geographical environments that you have been in. You have to make a change; you have to decide whether you want to live in the pigpen or victory.

While we are dealing with this account, let me further illustrate the principle of the power of positive confession. Remember, death and life are in the power of the tongue. In other words, in our words we hold the success of our future:

Let's look at verses 14-19 again:

14   *"But when he had spent all, there arose a severe famine in that land, and he began to be in want.*

15   *"Then he went and joined himself to a citizen of that country, and he sent him into his fields to feed swine.*

16   *"And he would gladly have filled his stomach with the pods that the swine ate, and no one gave him anything.*

17   *"But when he came to himself, he said* [Death and life are in the power of the tongue!) *'How many of my father's hired servants have bread enough and to spare, and I perish with hunger!*

18   *'I will arise and go to my father, and will say to him, "Father, I have sinned against heaven and before you,*

19   *"and I am no longer worthy to be called your son. Make me like one of your hired servants."*

Verse 17 does not say he *thought*. It says *he said* something. What did he say?

18   *'I will arise and go to my father, and will say to him, "Father, I have sinned against heaven and before you,*

19   *"and I am no longer worthy to be called your son. Make me like one of your hired servants."*

What did he do next? Did he remain in the pigpen the rest of his life? No! He arose and came to his father. He did something. You have to back up the words of your mouth with your life— actions. Your life has to correspond to your words, and then, what your mouth says will become a reality in your life. You have to *do* something!

153

You can arise today. I do not care where you are. I do not care if you are in the pigpens of life. I do not care if you are feeding swine, you can come out of that place, but you will have to arise. You will have to come to yourself and make a confession of faith and then act on that confession.

You have to say, "What am I doing wasting my life here? I am a child of the King of kings! I have been born again, and filled with the Holy Spirit. I have been living below my privileges. I have been letting the devil dictate the terms of my life, and I am going to arise and go to my heavenly Father."

How do you do that? You do it by confessing the Word of God. This is your right and privilege and you have it in Jesus.

CHAPTER ELEVEN

FACT 3A:

WHAT WE POSSESS IN CHRIST

We must confess *what we possess in* Christ if we are to live the overcoming and victorious life that Christ came to bring us. This has to deal with our inheritance. Whether you realize it or not, as a child of God, you have an inheritance. You have something that was left to you by a very rich person.

If you are poor, you usually do not leave a will, because you have nothing to bequeath to anyone. When you leave a will, it means an estate that you want disposed of after your demise, and you specifically want it to go to your heirs.

Well, Jesus Christ left a will. In fact, it is the book we call the Bible. The New Testament is actually the last will and testament of the Lord Jesus Christ. It is a legal document ratified by the High Court of Heaven, and Jesus is the executive administrator of the will. However, God cannot execute the will if the heirs do not cooperate. The heirs cannot cooperate if the heirs do not know they are heirs. If they do not know they have an inheritance, how can they claim it? How are you going to benefit from it when you do not know you have one?

Satan keeps most Christians in bondage to some degree at least, and whips their heads and kicks their backsides, because they do not know what they have and, therefore, cannot claim their inheritance. Satan had me in bondage for years. I thought my head was a punching bag. He whipped me every way but loose. And, what made it worse, Satan is so clever that he had me thinking that God was doing it.

The churches that I attended said the Lord was testing me. As a result, I ended up struggling, walking the streets of my city without a job, could not pay my bills, could not take care of my family, and I thought it was all a part of what was normal as a Christian.

We need to recognize that we do have an inheritance in Jesus. If we do not acknowledge and act on our inheritance, Satan is going to steal everything we have. He is going to usurp our rights and privileges, and leave us on welfare, as he has been doing to multitudes of Christians.

I am going to say something that will be considered controversial in the traditional church world, but I challenge you to challenge your own minister with what I am going to say. Watch his face, his expression, his eyes, and tell him not to give you a lot of theological mumbo jumbo. You ask him to show you in the Bible, chapter and verse, in English, that what I am going to say is not true. Do not just take his word, and don't take mine.

We have an inheritance and part of our inheritance is that we do not have to be sick. When I go back in my mind, I remember people in the church I knew who loved the Lord—and I am not talking about the elderly, I am speaking of people in the prime of life who died of debilitating diseases because they did not know they had an inheritance, guaranteeing them divine healing and health. The devil took advantage of them, of their ignorance and stole their lives from them. I watched those people die.

However, just because somebody died does not mean that was God's will. You cannot use that rationale, because if you do, you would have to say that it is God's will when somebody dies unsaved and goes to hell. We know from the Bible that it is not God's will for people to go to hell. God's Word says in John 3:16, *"that whoever believes in Him* [Jesus] *should not perish but have everlasting life."* The Bible did not say that God gave His Son because He so loved a certain segment of humanity. No! The Bible says, for God so loved the world that He gave His only begotten Son. However, there is a qualifier: that whoever believes in Him [Jesus] should not perish but have everlasting life.

If you do not claim your inheritance that is not God's fault. God provided it for you, but Satan, if given the chance, will steal it from you. He will steal your health, well-being, family, prosperity and all that is good.

Part of your inheritance is divine health. The ultimate goal is divine health, not divine healing. Divine healing is simply a pathway to divine health. God's best is health, not healing. Thank God for the healing that can catapult you into the health, but the best is to walk in health and not need healing. However, you cannot take advantage of your inheritance if you do not know what is due you. Then once you know your rights and privileges you must claim them by confessing them as yours. Yes, confess your right to healing right in the midst of the 105-degree temperature.

I am not telling you not to go to the doctor. I am saying that in order to activate your covenant, you have to confess God's promises. In the final analysis, it is still God who has to do the healing. For instance, if you break a bone; the doctor cannot make the bone grow back together. He can set it in the cast, but then he has to step away, fold his arms and wait for the body that God created to do its job and mend.

God wants you well. We can be healed and then learn how to cooperate with the things that God has set in motion, eat the right kinds of food, take care of our body and not give the devil a place. The Bible warns us not to give the devil a place. This means you have to take care of yourself; otherwise, you will give the devil an opportunity to place sickness or a disease on you. You cannot mistreat your body and then expect it to work as it was designed. When you do that you open the door for the enemy to come in like a flood to kill, steal and destroy. When you take care of your body, you minimize the attacks of Satan and their effects on you. You have to deal with the attacks because they are going to come, but they don't have to take hold, if you have been following God's Word—spirit, soul and body.

I will wager that you have known someone who was a Christian who died before their time. When I say before their time, I mean before they were 70 years old. God said, *My people are destroyed for lack of knowledge* (Hosea 4:6). We need to know what our inheritance is and then act on it.

We have a right to healing. We have a right to health. We have a right to joy. We have a right to peace. These things have been provided for you by Jesus, but you have to know it and appropriate it by faith. The way you do that is by a combination of (1) confessing the promises of God—speaking them over your life; (2) by buttressing that with a lifestyle that corresponds to what you say with your mouth.

In most of our churches, we are taught that the things of God are for when we get to heaven. It is all about what we are going to get in the future, over there on the other side, in the sweet by-and-by. However, I am here to tell you that according to the Word of God, you can have the sweet now-and-now because you are the child of the Most High God.

If you read the four Gospels, it is very interesting to note that Jesus did not come down here and encase Himself in a plastic bubble and have His disciples roll Him along for three and a half years up and down the roads of Palestine. We read time and time again where He went into people's homes and had a meal. In fact, He was so accustomed to doing that, the religious leaders said, "He eats with publicans and sinners." In fact, He got a reputation as a wine bibber because He was always with the people.

Jesus came down here and lived where we have to live, and the purpose of that was to show us that God is a very present help in the everyday life that we live, and not off in the future. God is interested in us now. This is why the Bible says that Jesus came to seek and to save the lost. Jesus came down right into the midst of us. He lived among us, walked among us, experienced the things that people went experienced, and was moved by it. When Lazarus died, the Bible says, Jesus wept. Jesus was a man of compassion who went about preaching, teaching and healing. Jesus did what He did to show us how to live in our inheritance.

When I found out that Jesus not only saved me from sin, but He saved me from sickness, disease, poverty, fear and any other negative thing that would destroy me and take my life, I got mad. I got righteously indignant. I got just as mad as Jesus got when He went into the temple and made that whip and chased those money changers out of His Father's house. He whipped them out of there—He became righteously indignant.

When I found out about my inheritance, I got mad at the church, mad at the preacher. I got mad at religion because they lied to me. I trusted my life to them and they lied to me. I thought they could be trusted. Now, I only trust the Bible. I will listen to what you have to say, but you will need to tell me where it came from so that I can check it out, because I want to be sure you know how to read. You may have read it wrongly. I cannot take any chances. My life is at stake!

ALL THINGS ARE YOURS

I got cheated out of seventeen years of my covenant rights. However, when I found out the truth, I determined that if anybody on the planet was going to have the benefits of the inheritance; it was going to be me.

Let me give you a scriptural example of your inheritance from First Corinthians 3:21:

> *Therefore let no one boast in men. For all*
> *things are yours:*

Underline the words *all things.* It did not say *all spirituals.* It says *things.* Is an automobile a thing? Is furniture a thing? Is jewelry a thing? Are clothes things? Are houses and lands and money things? God said *all things.* All means "everything without exception, nothing left out."

Notice, what it does not say. It does not say all things are God's. It says all things are yours. Paul is writing to every individual person in the family of God. We could personalize it and say *all things are mine.*

First Corinthians 3:22:

> *whether Paul or Apollos or Cephas, or the world*
> *or life or death, or things present or things to*
> *come; all are yours.*

What does it mean, *Paul is yours*? Paul is yours because Paul did not receive the revelations that he received from God only for his personal benefit. Paul received those revelations from God, so that he might communicate them to the Body of Christ. Then in the process of communicating them, Paul would also get the benefit and privilege to use them in his life.

Who does the world belong to? According to First Corinthians 3:22, it belongs to us. We have been lied to. We have been told we are just victims of the circumstances. However, God tells us that the world belongs to us. What does that mean? Does that mean you can go out and indiscriminately grab a block of land and say, "This is mine, and it belongs to me?" No! It means that God has given us gifts and talents to get the wealth, so that we can obtain those things that will enhance our lives. Because the world belongs to us!

Psalm 115:16 says:

> *The heaven, even the heavens, are the Lord's; but*
> *the earth He has given to the children of men.*

God created this world for us, His children. If He gave us the earth, then everything in the earth belongs to us. The good thing about this is that when God gives it to you, He gives it to you all the way, from the surface all the way down to the core.

We have another witness that tells us the world belongs to in Genesis 1:26:

> *Then God said, "Let Us make man in Our*
> *image, according to Our likeness; let them*
> *have dominion* [Dominion means lordship, rulership, caretaker-ship, oversight, ownership. It means you are in charge!] *over the fish of the sea, over the birds of the air, and over the cattle, over all the earth and over every creeping thing that creeps on the earth."*

We are supposed to have dominion. This is how God created us. This is what our possession is. Our possession is not waiting for us when we get to heaven, but is ours in this life on earth.

First Corinthians 3:22 also tells us that life belongs to the child of God. It is a precious possession—life! Then it says, not only life, but death is ours. Now, what does that mean? We have been led to believe, from traditional Christianity, that God is the author of death; that God may just decide to indiscriminately kill people or take them out of here.

There Is No Set Time for You to Die

We have all heard this thing about every man has a time to die. No, he does not. You are going to die for sure, but there is no set time for you to die. God does not have some chart up in heaven with everybody's name on it and the date they are going to die, regardless of what you do or what you say. If that were true, then the Bible would be invalidated. We would have to get rid of most of the Bible, because the promises of God are not based upon the fact that God has some set time for you die.

Because God is God, He is omniscient and knows all things, He knows when everybody is going to die, but He is not responsible for them dying at that time. Do you understand that? We are going to die. The Bible very clearly tells us that in Hebrews 9:27: *And as it is appointed for men to die once, but after this the judgment.*

There is an appointment that you have with death, but we have never been informed that we ought to make the appointment. We have been laboring under the delusion that God arbitrarily makes the appointment and there is nothing we can do about it.

As I said, if this were true, it would invalidate so much of the Bible. Because there are many promises in the Bible that have to do with our choice about how long we live, and it is not left up to God.

For instance, part of the 91st Psalm says, *With long life I will satisfy him, and show him My salvation.* Who will be satisfied? *He who dwells in the secret place of the Most High shall abide under the shadow of the Almighty.* What is long life? Long life, my friend, is not 35 years, 16 years, or 8 years. These ages cannot be considered long life because God says the minimum age we should live is 70 years.

God also told us in Exodus 20:12: *Honor your father and your mother, that your days may be long upon the land which the LORD your God is giving you.* Why would God hold out a promise like that to me, and then take me out at age 25? He would be lying to me. God said, with long life. . ., but if you do not know this part of your inheritance you will drop your guard and assume that it is inevitable. You allow fate to do its work and without realizing it, Satan operates within those confines and comes against you and destroys you. Then we end up blaming God for it.

God is not taking anybody by death. There are only three people God ever took, and in all three cases God took them alive —Enoch, Elijah and Jesus. They all left here alive, not dead. Life is yours and so is death!

GOD SHALL SUPPLY ALL YOUR NEED

Many people have reduced God down to the level of some super cosmic idea and believe that everything out there is in Star Trek land. However, God is very interested in what you will be experiencing in the practical issues of your day-to-day life. God is the God of the all.

In Philippians 4:19 the Word says:

> *And my God shall supply all your need according to His riches* [not according to my poverty, my empty wallet, or my empty bank account) *in glory* [How?] *by Christ Jesus.*

If God supplies all your need that means none of your needs are left out. You do not have any needs. Many people do not understand that and say, "I am not going to give Fred Price any money because he does not have any needs." However, they have missed the point altogether. They do not understand what I am doing when I confess or say "I believe that all my needs are met." That is exactly what God says, and my confession is what causes the need to be met.

The scripture does not say, "God had supplied." It says, *God shall supply*, which means the need cannot be met until it becomes a need. The only thing that God has to supply is whatever it is you need. If you do not need it yet, God does not have to supply it yet, because there is nothing to supply.

When I confess that all my needs are met, I am saying it by faith. Remember, I am talking about a lifestyle of faith. Romans 1:17 says, *The just shall live by faith.* It is a life lived every second of every minute of every hour of every day of every week of every month of every year of every decade. Faith is not for isolated situations. It is a total lifestyle.

I have been operating by faith for more than 30 years, and I have not yet attained the plateau that I am planning to attain. I have not reached the top yet. I believe faith works; I teach it and confess it. Because of practicing this principle of positive confession all the time, I have come to a place in my life where I actually have no unmet needs. For years now, I have only been dealing with desires. We are admonished in Psalm 37:4 to do the following:

> *Delight yourself also in the LORD, and He*
> *shall give you the desires of your heart.*

Some people might say, "I'm not gonna give Fred Price anything, because he said he doesn't have any needs. But wait a minute! Do not deny me my desires. I do have some desires. Help me with the desires. One's needs are not the only things in life.

When I did not have a dollar in my pocket, I said, "Praise God, my God supplies all my need according to His riches in glory by Christ Jesus." Understand that God's Word is not true because you are experiencing the promises. It is true because God said it. Because God said it and you believe and confess it that is what produces the results. This is what causes it to come to pass in your life.

The scripture did not say that my God shall supply all my need, when I can figure out how God is going to do it. It says, My God shall supply. . . . I have to believe that and confess it. When I confess it, put action to it, that is my faith talking and that opens the channel for God's Word to manifest in my life.

God can show Himself mighty once He has a channel. If you limit Him by trying to figure out with your little pea-sized brain how He is going to do it, then you will limit His power in your life. I have been speaking life to my life for more than 30 years, and I have been building up reserves. This is how it works, and as it builds up. You end up with abundance beyond your needs.

When you get to this point of abundance you become the "need provider" for other people because ultimately, all needs are met through people. Money does not fall out of the sky. I have never, personally, received any money from out of the sky and neither have you. Every dollar that has come to me has been because some person was inspired to give to me. It was God speaking to them, directing them, because of my faith confession.

For example, God meets the needs of the local church that I pastor through the obedience of the people who tithe and give offerings. No money has fallen out of the sky in all the years I have been pastor of Crenshaw Christian Center. It all comes through the hands of man in the form of offerings.

In the natural, it is crazy to give away money you have worked for. You give it to God and you cannot see Him. This is unintelligent if you look at it academically. If you look at it spiritually, you understand what it is — being obedient to the Word of God, and through that, He meets the needs of the person giving.

This is what you possess. You have a right to have your needs met. You have to also understand that there are some parameters that govern and control the meeting of those needs. For instance, for the 30 years that I have been giving, I have been paying tithes—not out of duty, but out of love, because I wanted to be obedient.

Thank God that He commanded me to do something I can do. If He had told me to run 500 miles an hour, I would not make it. If He had told me to make straight A's on all my school tests, I would have flunked out and missed His blessings. If He had told me to climb to the top of Mount Everest, I could not have done that. However, He gave me something I could do. Give 10 percent of my income, and then of course, give offerings, and I gladly give both.

As I began to give, it got so good I started giving more than what God asked; not because I felt any coercion to do it, but just because I decided I wanted to do it. I wanted to because I had cheated God for so many years in this area of giving. I said, "I want to make my amends," not out of guilt, but just because I could. So, I began giving 25 percent of my income and my giving has increased since then. Today, because of the great abundance my giving has produced, my wife and I give 40 percent of our income to the Kingdom, and we are not lacking in any area of our lives.

My wife and I are able to give so much because I started operating in these spiritual laws when we had little to give. If you keep planting good seed in good ground and taking care of the ground, harvest is assured. God has built a harvest into every seed, but the seed has to be planted correctly.

As I began planting seed, the harvest began coming. This is why giving is so important. You not only have to confess the Word, but you have to do the Word. In Malachi the Word says, *"Will a man rob God?"* The people said, *"How have we robbed You?"* God said, *"In tithes and offerings."* What is so peculiar to me is that people will balk at paying a 10 percent tithe. I mean, they get upset! "I don't see why I gotta pay a 10 percent tithe," but have no quarrels with paying up to a 25 percent interest rate for the privilege of using a bank card. They will pay that much interest to strangers, but balk at paying their own heavenly Father 10 percent tithes.

RECONCILING SPIRITUAL AND MATERIAL THINGS

According to God's Word, I am already blessed. We possess blessings, not curses, as a result of being in Christ. Blessings are part of our inheritance.

Ephesians 1:3:

> *Blessed be the God and Father of our Lord Jesus Christ, who has blessed* [Underline the words "has blessed"] *us with every* [Underline the word *every*] *spiritual blessing in the heavenly places in Christ.*

The word *has* is past tense, which indicates that the time of action has already taken place. It is not in the process of taking place. It is not going to take place someday off in the distant future. *Has blessed* is past tense—already done.

According to the scripture we just read, we are blessed with *all*. All is an inclusive term. No blessing is left out. Now, here is the dilemma. "It is great that I am blessed with all spiritual blessings but, Lord, my roof is leaking. This is not a spiritual need. Lord, I have bald tires on my car. The tread on my tires are so thin, I can see the cord. Thank You, Lord, for blessing me spiritually, but I need some tires for my car. This need is material, not spiritual. Lord, I thank You for blessing me with all spiritual blessings in heavenly places in Christ, but did You know my property tax bill just came? This bill is not spiritual. Lord, I need some money to pay my property taxes!"

A legitimate question at this time would be, "How do you reconcile these spiritual and material things?" By going back to Jesus. Jesus is the reason. He is the foundation head of it all. Jesus is where it begins. The question again is, "How are these spiritual blessings translated into material blessings in everyday life?" The answer is a simple biblical truth. What we have to do is go back and think of things in terms of origin. We need to go back to the beginning, back to Genesis. I want to show you the process that the Spirit of God showed me so you can understand the relationship between the spiritual and the material.

When I first was confronted with the verse in Ephesians, *Blessed be the God and Father of our Lord Jesus Christ, who has blessed us with every spiritual blessing. . .,* I had the economic wolf on my front porch, and God was talking about spiritual blessings. I needed money, honey! How does that verse translate into money? The Lord showed me how it does in Genesis 1:1: *In the beginning God created the heavens and the earth.*

Question: What are the heavens (the solar system) and the earth? Are they spiritual or material things? They are material, of course. Question: Which came first, God or the earth? It was God, of course. Then God must be more real than the heaven and the earth He created, right?

Let us take another step toward our solution. John 4:24 says, *God is a Spirit. . . .* Now look at John 1:1: *In the beginning was the Word, and the Word was with God, and the Word was God.* The word *Word* in the Greek is logos, and that word means or refers to Jesus, or the Son of God, or Christ, or Messiah, or the second person in the Godhead. It said, *in the beginning.* This sounds similar to Genesis 1: *In the beginning God . . . .* John 1: *In the beginning was the Word. . . . .*

Genesis 1: *In the beginning God created. . . .* John 1: *In the beginning was the Word . . . .*

If anybody ought to know what God is, Whoever was with God in the beginning ought to know. Jesus was there and He says that God is a Spirit.

Earlier I asked you if the earth was material or spiritual, and we determined that it is material. If that is true and God created it, and Jesus said that God is a Spirit, then that means that a Spirit created material things. This tells us that this Spirit must be more real than the material things He created. The Bible documents that everything that is material had its origin in the spirit realm. This means that material things are dependent upon spiritual things for their existence, which confirms the idea that everything starts in the Spirit realm.

When the scripture says, *Blessed be the God and Father of our Lord Jesus Christ, who has blessed us with every spiritual blessing in the heavenly places in Christ,* it means that the leaky roof was first of all spiritual. It means that those four bald tires were first of all spiritual. It means the money I need to pay my taxes was first of all spiritual, because it was a Spirit that created material things. Can you understand this?

I have my new roof in Christ in heavenly places. I have my four new tires in heavenly places. I have money to pay my taxes in heavenly places. All I have to do is believe it and by faith bring it into the reality of this material world through my positive confession of God's Word, because every spiritual blessing is mine. Hallelujah!

It starts in the Spirit world and by faith is brought into the material three-dimensional world. This truth is awesome! Let us go back to Genesis 1:1-3:

1   *In the beginning God created the heavens and the earth.*

2   *The earth was without form, and void; and darkness was on the face of the deep. And the Spirit of God was hovering over the face of the waters.*

3   *Then God said, "Let there be light"; and there was light.*

Notice that there was no light until after God said *"Let there be light."* He had faith in His own words. This is why it takes faith to please God, because He is a faith God. He operates by faith.

171

God said . . . *let the dry land appear; and it was so.* Nothing came into existence until after God said it. He did it by the words of His mouth. This is how He created this material world that we live in. God was using the law of positive confession. He was speaking it into existence. If you want that new roof, talk it into existence. If you want those new tires, talk them into existence. If you want the money to pay your taxes, talk it into existence. You are already blessed. You already have your roof, tires, and tax money in heavenly places. Just speak them into existence. It works!

I really like what the Hebrew says about this. In the New King James translation, the Bible reads: *"Let there be light"; and there was light.* However, in the Hebrew language the real essence is that God said, *Light be and light was.* I like that—roof be, and roof was. Glory to God!

Again, Ephesians 1:3 tells us:

> *Blessed be the God and Father of our Lord Jesus*
> *Christ, who has blessed us with every spiritual*
> *blessing in the heavenly places in Christ,*

God has made an investment, a deposit, in Christ for us. We have to start with the spiritual and bring them, by our faith, into the physical three-dimensional world. This is why God says we are "blessed with all spiritual blessings."

According to God's Word, all of our needs are met. By faith, we must confess it, and then, of course, line up with all of the other things that God's Word declares that we ought to do. When we do, we can expect, absolutely, positively, unequivocally, that all of our needs will be met and manifested in due season—if we faint not, but stand on God's unchanging Word.

CHAPTER TWELVE

FACT 3B:
WHAT WE POSSESS IN CHRIST
—FEAR NOT

W hat else do we possess in Christ?

Second Timothy 1:7 declares:

> For God has not given us a spirit of fear, but
>
> of power and of love and of a sound mind.

The scripture tells us that fear is a spirit. Fear is an unnatural

thing for mankind. God did not create us with fear potential. What

happened was that when Adam sinned man died spiritually—died in the sense of being cut off from God—mankind was left with only the flesh or soul to guide them.

FEAR NOT

Satan, the god of this world, operates in the realm of the flesh and soul. He sends his demon spirits to torment man with all kinds of fears. And, because most Christians do not know their authority in Christ they allow the fears to take hold of them. God has not given us the spirit of fear, because there is no fear in God and He cannot give us what He does not have.

This kind of fear is paralyzing. This kind of fear seems to come over you in given situations. In such situations, you lose contact with reality, and in some cases, even freeze up, unable to move and you become helpless. This is not of God.

I am not talking about reverential fear, or respect. For instance, I have a water heater in my house. This gas water heater has a pilot light with fire in it. I am not afraid of fire, but I have great respect for it. I know that I should not put my hands in the fire because I could burn my hands. To have respect for something is one thing, but to be so afraid that you cannot carry on daily activities is another story. Know this: that your newborn, re-created human spirit comes from God and God does not send anything down here with fear in it.

Even as a Christian, fears can come into your flesh, into your mind, and control your life. If you do not know your rights in Christ and learn how to confess God's Word, that demonic spirit of fear will overtake you. You have to learn how to resist fear, just like you would resist somebody taking something away from you in the natural. You resist fear with your confession and with your stand of faith. I had to learn how to do this very thing.

All of my life, as far as my conscious remembrance goes, I was afraid of water, afraid of it in the sense of putting my head under water. I only have little snatches of memory that something negative occurred. My father had a drinking problem. He would get drunk and do some crazy things. I vaguely remember we were at the beach during a holiday. He had been drinking. He picked me up and put me on his shoulders. I was just a little fellow at the time, and my legs dangled around his neck. He started out into the water and I was petrified. I kept hollering, "No! No! No!" We kept getting deeper and deeper into the water until it came up to where I was. I do not know whether he dropped me or whether he put me in. This part is a blank. However, ever since that time, I had a fear of putting my head under the water. In fact, I could not get my head close to the water, not even standing in the shower.

If I was taking a shower and happened to turn my head the wrong way and water went up my nose, I would begin to gag and gasp for breath. I felt smothered, or claustrophobic. Think about it, a grown man, and I never had my head under water until I was forty years old. I would not go swimming. In fact, I used to watch Jacques Cousteau on television—loved to see the undersea world and I wanted to go underwater. I thought, "Boy that is wonderful. What a blessing to be able to go underwater and see all the undersea world that God has created." Then, I would begin thinking about putting my head under water and fear would start creeping all over me.

Some of you have had—or have fears like I had. Examples of such fears can include: close places like an elevator, going into tall buildings, or in high places. All these fears—we call them phobias—are not natural and they do not come in the genes. They are learned. These spirits can become a part of you as a child and affect you the rest of your life if you allow them. However, you have to overcome them with the Word of God and your faith confessions.

I found out from God's Word that He did not give me the spirit of fear; I did not have to be afraid of anything. I made a statement one time in a sermon, that by faith, I had overcome all the fears I ever had—except for the fear of putting my head under water. I said, "I am going to learn how to swim. Up till now, I have not had the time to do it, and I do not have a swimming pool." Two members of my church heard me make this statement and offered me their swimming pool and provided me with their swimming instructor, free of charge. This made it convenient for me, and I went to their home and learned how to swim. I overcame that fear with my faith, applying God's Word to my situation.

Shortly thereafter, I had a pool put in my yard. Then I said, "I am going to learn how to scuba dive." I became a certified scuba diver. I did the same thing with flying on airplanes. For years, I would not fly on an airplane. You could not get me on an airplane. You could not shoot me, handcuff me, put me in a coffin and get me on an airplane. I would resurrect! I was terrified of flying on airplanes and yet I loved them. It was really not the fear of airplanes; it was the fear of death. I had to learn that the Lord had delivered me from the fear of death.

Thank God I found out that God had not given me the spirit of fear. You have to know that and confess it. It will take some time, and you will not lose that fear overnight. If you have been afraid of something for forty years, you will not lose that fear by snapping your fingers. You have to fight it, and you have to stand against it.

The Bible says in Ephesians 6:12: *For we do not wrestle against flesh and blood, but against principalities, against powers, against the rulers of the darkness of this age, against spiritual hosts of wickedness in the heavenly places.* It is a battle, a fight, and it is very real.

I remember one time as the pastor of a small church, I had to go to a meeting in Chicago (from Los Angeles), to represent my little pastorate. I did not have much time to get there, and there was only one practical way to go. You guessed it—by airplane!

I had a friend, a businessman, who flew all the time. He was telling me all of the advantages of flying first-class as opposed to flying coach or tourist class. He told me that his company would provide him with a coach ticket and then, for a few more dollars, he would pay the difference himself and ride first-class. So, I decided to travel first-class, since this was my first flight.

I went to the airport, shaking all the way there. I will not lie to you, my palms were sweaty. I was afraid, but there was nothing I could do. I had to go and I could not refuse to go without revealing how scared I really was. I had to play it cool. Here I was, leading people, telling them what to do, and I was scared myself!

The flight was supposed to depart at 10 o'clock. I am a very punctual person, so I assume everybody else is, too. Well, 10 o'clock came, then 10:05, then 10:10, and the plane had not moved. I was really getting nervous now. I had psyched myself up to fly, and now they were late. All kinds of thoughts began to run through my mind as to why they were late. Finally, the captain came over the loudspeaker and said, "Ladies and gentlemen, we are experiencing a few technical difficulties." This is all I needed to hear—*something is wrong with the plane!* I thought, "You must be kidding. My first flight and you have mechanical problems?" My stomach was turning over on the inside. At about 10:15, the plane still had not moved. I broke out in a cold sweat. At about 10:20, the pilot came back on the intercom, "Ladies and gentlemen, we believe that we have located our problem and the mechanics will be moving towards that problem in a few moments to fix it. We should be airborne in approximately 10 to 15 minutes. Thank you very much for your patience."

Two mechanics approached the plane with a ladder and toolbox. Think about this: Here is a four-engine airplane. You have four great possibilities of mechanical problems in the engines—two engines on the right side and two engines on the left side. Why couldn't it be one of the engines on the left side of the plane? No, it had to be one of the engines on the right side of the plane—where I was sitting! These two sets of engines are called the inboard engine and the other outboard. The outboard engine is camouflaged by the inboard engine. To further my distress, Satan made sure that it was the inboard engine—right outside my window that needed repair!

The mechanics went to work with their ladder up to the engine, peering inside. One of the men took a screwdriver from his toolbox. I could see the engine parts gleaming in the sunlight, like the organs of the human body. I was thinking the mechanic, like some famous heart surgeon, was going to deftly insert the screwdriver into those engine innards, like a surgeon would into the human body. No, instead he jabs it into those engine parts like he was chipping ice with an ice pick.

Inside, I was screaming. No! What are you doing? Stop! By this time, I am wiping sweat off my face. I was absolutely petrified. Fear was all over me—God's great man of faith and power. Finally, they finished. We left one hour late. By this time I was totally out of it. I could not have been more out of it if I had taken 500 ounces of heroin. I had overdosed on fear!

At this time, I did not know that much about automatic pilots. I did not know that once the plane reached cruising altitude, they put the plane on automatic pilot. Periodically, the automatic pilot will make adjustments for the course and you can feel a slight flutter or movement, especially if you are scared like I was. As you can imagine, I was extremely sensitive to every move, every sound, and every noise.

I was so scared that I sat in that seat with my eyes glued to the window. From Los Angeles to Chicago, I watched that engine all the way. I did not take my eyes off that engine. I was traveling first-class, so the stewardesses were coming down the aisles with those four-wheeled carts serving prime rib with all the trimmings. However, I did not eat or drink. I was so terrified I just watched that engine all the way to Chicago. Every time the plane fluttered or made a slight movement, I just knew that engine was going to fall off. Although, if it had fallen, what in the world could I have done about it? Fear is ridiculous. It does not make sense.

However, by coming into the truth of God's Word, I took my faith, as I did with the fear of water, and I overcame that fear of flying. As of today, I have flown tens of thousands of miles all over the world. As a matter of fact, I have been in some situations where it looked like the plane was going down, and I probably was the only one on board who was not afraid. No fear —none whatsoever. I took my faith and overcame the fear.

As a child of God, you have no legitimate reason to fear anything, because God is in you by His Holy Spirit. But you have to believe and you have to confess it. You have to say, "I believe I am not afraid." Then, keep right on pushing forward, and you will break that spirit of fear. Fear cannot stay with you if you will confess the Word of God over the situation. At first you may be like I was on the flight to Chicago, sweating all the way. However, just as I did, you can say by faith, "I believe everything is fine. I believe I am safe in the name of Jesus."

If we want to conquer fear, we must walk by faith and not by sight—we walk by the Word of God and not by what our senses are telling us. We have not been given the spirit of fear. We possess that in Christ. We do not have to be afraid of anything as a child of God. Now, use wisdom. If you drop something in the fire, do not reach inside unless the Spirit of God tells you to—and you had better know that it is the Spirit ot God telling you, like Shadrach, Meshach and Abednego in the Book of Daniel. You should have respect and use wisdom in all situations. However, you do not have to be afraid and you do not have to back off of anything in fear.

People are afraid of all kinds of things. But let me tell you how to break your fear, that spirit that comes against your mind and against your flesh. You have to face the fear in its own element in that very place where it says you are afraid with God's Word. The blessings of God are available to us to the extent that we are willing to confess that they are ours. The only way you will have those blessings in actual manifestation in your life is to confess them. This is what makes it work. With boldness you need to say, "I possess this because I am in Christ. I have a covenant right to it because the Word of God says so. God says so. Jesus says so, and I say so. I do not care who says I do not, Jesus says I do!"

The only person who can stop your blessings from coming is you. This is the wonderful thing about walking by faith. I encourage you to learn how to walk by your own faith. Do not get into the habit of having someone else agree with you. Do not misunderstand me. It is good that husbands and wives be on one accord. They should be in agreement, but the bottom line is this is between you and God's Word.

I want to share with you a very precious letter as an example of what we possess in Christ. It is a good example of the power of positive confession, how someone took a stand on God's Word, made their confession, and received their heart's desire. It says:

> *Dear Pastor Price:*
>
> *. . . My husband and I are new to Los Angeles and to Crenshaw. We are here because of the power of positive confession. For a number of years, while we lived in Dallas, we had studied with you. It was through your teachings that we first gained spiritual knowledge of Proverbs 18:21 and how faith works. As we studied with you and several other anointed teachers, our measure of faith was challenged in several areas, so we started putting our mustard seed faith out there. We began to change what we said. Instead of confessing everything that was going wrong, we started saying, "Father, we thank You that Your Word does not return to You empty, but it will accomplish what pleases You and achieve the purpose for which You sent it. We thank You that all of our needs are met according to Your riches in glory by Christ Jesus. We thank You that we can do all things through Christ who strengthens us and that no weapon formed against us can prosper."*
>
> *At first, we took real baby steps, oftentimes repeating these Bible confessions right behind you as we ran that tape back and forth. But with time, our steps strengthened, and our faith grew.*
>
> *We went from a seed to a bush, then to a hedge, and finally started to get the first braches on our faith tree. That brings us to Crenshaw. We had our first opportunity to fellowship at Crenshaw in July 1984. You did not make it to Dallas that year, so we decided we could get you and Disneyland in at the same time. We arrived that Friday evening and decided we'd go spy out*

that church that Saturday. We would be all set for Sunday.

We drove over to the old church and saw that "Moved" sign. So, we found Vermont Avenue. I must say we were not exactly prepared for 7901 South Vermont. We thought, "Boy! If faith can do this and more, we are gonna stick with this. The security officer was so very cordial and gave us all the information we needed for Sunday morning. As we arrived for the first service, our spirits got more and more excited. Even in the perimeters of the church, we sensed something was very different. And when we actually reached the campus, we knew we were on Holy ground.

Even though we had been studying with you quite a while, we felt just like children as we sat and listened to the Word which came forth, hanging on and gobbling up every word. One of the things we had always appreciated in you is the simplicity of the Word of God delivered through you.

When I listened to you teach I knew the truth of "For my yoke is easy and my burden is light. " I do not readily understand or receive what you may have taught during a particular lesson, but I thank God for His Word and the way in which you presented it to the Body. Thank you for K.l.S.S. That is my favorite principle of operation. K.l.S.S. — Keep it simple, saint!

When we returned to Dallas, our little spirits were really sagging. We knew in our hearts we wanted to be here, but we couldn't afford to be out of His will, so back to Dallas we went.

As we drove home from the airport that evening, we sat silently almost all the way. Then my husband said, "We're going to Los Angeles." A big grin came on my face and I said, "Yes, I know."

Then he said, "I don't know how we're going to get there, but we're going . . . ." We expressed to the Father our desire to come to Crenshaw and asked whether it was His will for our lives. A few days later, in the course of my daily Bible study, I came to the 8th chapter of Deuteronomy. It was like, Wow! Rhema!

I jumped up and ran to show *my husband. Immediately, we received it in our hearts as confirmation. We thanked God for it and immediately began confessing "We're going to Crenshaw!"*

Well, time passed, and it looked like nothing was happening at all, but everyday we kept saying, "Lord, we thank You that we're in fellowship with Pastor Price and Crenshaw." I think we started applying every principle and confession of faith that the Father had taught us through you.

Then one day, opportunity knocked! My husband received a new job offer. But there was one major hitch. We would have to relocate to where, of all places, Los Angeles! We nearly went through the roof! I think we danced in the Spirit for days!

We made our pre-move trip that spring and got everything ready to go, including putting our house on the market. I need not tell you that our adversary, the devil, was on *the job, too, and he threw out some major glitches, including a company restructuring that put virtually all activity on hold. But we kept thanking God that we are in fellowship with Pastor Price and Crenshaw. We knew that we were not alone. As the FaithDome rose in spite of Satan's attacks, our faith rose, too.*

Then, in November 1987, my husband came home and said, "We're going to L.A." I said, "Yes, I know." He said, "No! You're not listening to me. *We're going to Los Angeles!" Then it clicked.*

We're going to Los Angeles! We're going to Crenshaw. Fred, it had been almost four years, four whole years of believing and confessing. Even as the actual time for the move got closer, Satan kept verbally threatening us with things like, "Well, you know the company is starting to lay off people. It's awfully stupid to be going out there now with so many things up in the air. And on top of that, everything is so much more expensive. And wow, what about the crime! And besides that, you don't know what to do in an earthquake! Everybody is going to drop off into the ocean, you know."

It got ridiculous, but our reply was "No! None of that matters, because we have the victory. When they open the doors to the FaithDome for the first time, we're marching in with the family, yes!"

On Wednesday, September 28, 1988, the confession manifested as we became members of Crenshaw Christian Center! That was one of the most special times we will ever experience in our lives, because God granted the desires of our heart. As a matter of fact, I felt like it was graduation day all over again.

Unfortunately, it's easy for many saints to believe God for supplying our needs, but many times hold back their faith when it comes to our desires and miss the abundance that God has in store for us.

I am so happy that our family learned to believe and receive the truth that God is willing, not only to meet our needs, but to give us the desires of our hearts, too.

I am so glad that we chose to take heed to the Word of faith, because faith works. My husband has learned to take no thought in the affairs or our lives, and is now blessed more than we had believed in his new job. Our son attend Frederick K.C. Price School, which the Father raised up and anointed with the vision for excellence . . . .

This ministry is so much more than lights and cameras . . . . We are personally grateful for the TV ministry, for through it all, the seed of this desire was sown, watered, and nurtured to fullness. I can't overemphasize how very valuable Crenshaw Christian Center and Ever Increasing Faith are in the Body of Christ . . . . We thank the Lord Jesus Christ that He chose to call you, Pastor and Mrs. Price, not only servant, but friend. We love you. To God be all the glory, honor, majesty and power for ever and ever. Amen.

The Word works! Faith works! Confession works! Death and life are in the power of the tongue! I say it again, unless you are willing and faithful to press through with your confession and believe they are yours, you will not personally receive all of the provision and blessing that are available in the Word of God.

If a thief tried to take your belongings, would you resist? Of course you would. But it is amazing how Christians will let the devil take what belongs to them without any resistance. They roll over and play dead like a dog and let Satan take everything that belongs to them.

Satan is a thief and a robber, and you have to resist him. You have to stand against him or he will steal what belongs to you. Again, it is by faith that you stand against him. Christians will say, "Praise the Lord, if this is for me, I will get it. And if it is not for me, I won't." This kind of thinking and talking does not work. This is not biblically sound thinking.

Remember, the Bible says, *"It is not God's will that any should perish, but that all should come to repentance."* Why is it not God's will that any should perish? Because John 3:16 says, *"For God so loved the world that He gave His only begotten Son, that whoever believes in Him should not perish but have everlasting life."*

Even though it is not God's will that any perish, folk are perishing. Why? Because it is not up to God whether they perish or not, it is up to the individual. It is up to God to provide them a method by which they will not perish, but whether they perish or not is based upon their decision, their volitional faith act of taking advantage of what God has supplied.

Satan will steal from you every minute of every day unless you stand up and fight for your rights, and there is nothing God can do to stop him. The reason I say there is nothing God can do is because He has already done it. Now the responsibility is in your hands. He has given you all the tools necessary to do something about it. If I do not do the Word of God, that is my fault.

When my car was delivered from England, I was notified to come down to the dealer and pick up the car. When I did so, I was given the papers and the keys. I could have sat right there in the parking lot for the next ten years, if I had not acted. The dealership had done its part, and it was up to me to drive the car home. God, through His Word has delivered to you your "car." You have the owner's papers, the keys, license tags, everything. Now, it is up to you to drive it. If you do not drive it, you will sit there in the garage of your life and go nowhere.

John 10:10 tells us:

> *The thief does not come except to steal, and to kill, and to destroy. I have come that they may have life, and that they may have it more abundantly.*

The will of Jesus for me is a more abundant life. However, if I want it, I will have to confess it. You will never get it unless you confess it, because Satan will steal it from you. He will steal anything from you that he can.

Understand how he works: He does not walk into a room with a red suit on and a pitchfork in his hand and say, "I'm the devil and I'm here to steal your blessings." No, it will come through the system, through the circumstances.

Until you confess in faith that all of what God clearly declares is yours, you will never get it. Satan will keep you spiritually and materially bound; poor and without the things that constitute abundant life. I do not know how confession works, and I do not really care. I am just glad that it works for anyone who commits to it.

WORRYING IS SIN

First Peter 5:7 says:

> *Casting all your care upon Him, for He cares for you.*

If you are a caring person, you have things that concern you—children, parents, wife, husband, families, jobs, professions, and homes. These things do not always work correctly, so they cause concern and sometimes that concern gets right down to worry.

Many people, including Christians, operate in constant, ongoing worry. They are so concerned until it affects their ability to function on a daily basis. First Peter 5:7 is a scripture we should confess. It we do not, Satan will steal our peace of mind.

The word *casting* means to "throw away from you." This scripture tells us to cast all our cares on the Lord—so how much is left out of "all"? None! It is interesting that most Christians would never think of drinking a can of beer or a cocktail, because they consider that to be sinful. They would never steal anything, because they would consider that to be a sin. However, they worry constantly and think nothing about it being a sin.

The reason they think it is not wrong is because everybody worries, generally speaking, and since they do, it is an accepted method of dealing with the issues of life. However, it is a sin to worry! Why? Because when I worry, I am calling God a liar, I am saying, "Heavenly Father, Your Word is not good. You do not care about Your children."

If you believe that God has handled the matter, why would you be worrying? Worrying is your attempt to do something about the situation, which means you are not satisfied to let God do it. Worry is a lack of trust. It is a lack of faith in God's Word.

I used to be a world champion worrier. In fact, I worried so much until I worried a hole in my stomach, called a peptic ulcer. I could not eat and keep any food in my stomach. I worried all the time. I worried about everything and was uptight all the time. I was trying to solve all my problems, and they were too big tor me.

When I found out how to walk by faith, I retired from worrying! When I found out how to walk in accord with God's Word, some 30 years ago, I stopped worrying. Do not misunderstand me, there are things for which I am responsible, things I am accountable for, but I do not worry about them. I do my part, and then leave it in the hands of the Lord. For instance, the FaithDome; it took from July, 1977 to July, 1986—nine years—to get in position to build the Dome. Then it took an additional three years to actually construct it. If it had been me building that Dome, it would have been built in a year. I would have worked 24 hours a day on it. But I could not do it and I knew it. I did not lose any sleep over it. I resigned myself to the fact that if it never got finished, it was not my problem, it was God's.

I did my part. The rest was up to the Lord to work through people to get the job done. I cast all my care on Him because He cares for me. I confessed that the FaithDome was built, and I did not worry one second through it all.

If you are still worried, you have not cast it on Him. God will not get involved until you cast it on Him. Now Satan will back you into a corner if you let him, saying, "What are you going to do if so-and-so does not happen?" "What will people say if they come and repossess your car?" You have to resist him and fight him with his tactics. For instance, tell him. "I'll tell you what they will say, devil: They repossessed my car. So what? That is not the last car they will make. I will get another one."

If you know how to believe God, your car will not be repossessed. What I am saying is that you must learn to fight the devil on his terms, or else he will intimidate you with worry. Confession must become a way of life if you want to enjoy and experience what we have in Christ. In order for this to work on the highest level, you have to be consistent, faithful, unmovable, unshakable and unbendable.

Matthew 8:17 tells us something else that we possess in Christ:

> *that it might be fulfilled which was spoken by Isaiah the prophet, saying: "He Himself took our infirmities and bore our sicknesses."*

This verse of scripture is referring to Jesus, who took our infirmities and bore our sicknesses. It is obvious that if Jesus bore my sicknesses, He does not want me to bear them. Therefore, I retired from sicknesses and disease 30 years ago. Illness does not belong to me.

This does not mean you are not going to be attacked because that is what Ephesians 6:11,13 is all about when it says, *Put on the whole armor of God, that you may be able to stand against the wiles of the devil. . . . Therefore take up the whole armor of God, that you may be able to withstand in the evil day, and having done all, to stand.* Why? Because the darts are going to come. Sickness and disease are some of the darts. If you are a Christian, then you have a right to be well. It is not God's will for you to be sick. Many Christians have strange ideas. They figure that if you do not get sick or get killed in some kind of calamity, how are you going to die? Well, have you ever thought about wearing out? You do not have to get sick to die. Divine healing and divine health are your possession, but you have to confess it.

When I feel bad, I do not confess I feel bad, but I confess I believe I am healed. I do not deny that I am feeling bad, but rather, I do not talk about it.

Second Corinthians 4:18:

> *while we do not look at the things which are seen, but at the things which are not seen. For the things which are seen are temporary, but the things which are not seen are eternal.*

God did not say that the things that are seen do not exist. He said, do not look at them. If you do not look at them, what do you do? Ignore them. How do you do that? The same way you ignore a person when you don't want to be bothered. Ignore the sickness the same way. Act as if it is not there. You do not say it is not there. When you ignore someone, you are not saying that they are not there.   You are just not giving them any credit for having anything to do with you at that moment in time. This is what you have to do with sickness and disease.

What I have said is not some kind of psychological, mental approach. It is a spiritual law. Just because we have never heard something before does not invalidate it or make it cultish, or something out of line with the Word of God.

I have been married for more than 50 years, and I did not find out about the law of confession until after the first 17 years of my marriage. I operated in that law of confession all those years. However, the first 17 years were lived in a negative environment created by my own confession. Instead of governing what I said with my mouth, I said whatever I felt, whatever I saw, and whatever I could figure out with my mind. I did not confess what the Word said about the situation.

Now that I look back on it, it is interesting to see that I actually experienced in my everyday life the sum total of what I had been negatively confessing, You have to understand that laws work whether you know they are working or not. Although you may not know that there is such a thing as the law of confession, it does not make any difference, it is working anyway. If you are on the negative side of the law, it will work for you in a negative way and produce negative results in your life and you cannot blame God. You control your circumstances by your confession, and that, of course, should be based on your faith in the Word of God.

At the beginning of this book, I told you that we are whatever the Word of God says we are, whether we are experiencing that or not. If God says we have it, we have it. Whatever God says we can do, we can do. However, if you do not get in line with God's estimate of you, you will go down below the level of who you really are and there is nothing God can do about it. Because He has already done all He is going to do through Christ. I have to know my covenant rights, believe them, confess them, and then they will begin to operate in my life.

Matthew 8:17 says:

> *that it might be fulfilled which was spoken*
> *by Isaiah the prophet, saying: "He Himself*
> *took our infirmities and bore our sicknesses."*

You need to make that personal. It says "our," but our means the Body of Christ. I am a member of the Body of Christ, so I could reduce this down to a personal level. Jesus took *my* infirmities, so that means He does not want me to have them.

Romans 5:17 of the Amplified Bible reads:

> *For if because of one man's trespass (lapse,*
> *offense) death reigned through that one, much*
> *more surely will those who receive [God's]*
> *overflowing grace (unmerited favor) and the free*
> *gift of righteousness [putting them into right*
> *standing with Himself] reign as kings in life*
> *through the one Man Jesus Christ (the Messiah,*
> *the Anointed One).*

He said I should reign in life as a king, not as a welfare recipient. I am to reign in life, not in heaven, not in the sweet by-and-by, over there on the other side, after while, but over here on this side of life. God said I should reign as a king in life! Christianity has been sold a bill of goods. The Church of the Lord Jesus Christ, by and large, operates on the basis of the poverty syndrome. The devil told us that we are supposed to be poor in this life, because we are going to get our wealth over on the other side, but this is not true.

The Bible says that it is impossible for God to lie, so the only alternative is that God must tell the truth. Therefore, if God tells me that I am a king, I must be a king. When I first found this out, I did not look like one and I sure had nothing that would place me in a kingly category. But I began to see myself sitting on a throne—the throne of my own life, not reigning and ruling over somebody else and dictating to them, but reigning over my own life.

I began to see myself that way, even when I did not have a dime, and could not pay my bills. I was struggling; my struggles had struggles! But I began to see myself as a king. I began to see the blessings of God pouring out on me. Since I am a king, I should be treated as a king. I should receive tribute like a king receives tribute.

Example: I was sitting in my office one day minding my own business. A minister called and made an appointment to see me through my secretary. He had some questions about ministry that he wanted to ask me. He asked me his questions and then before leaving, he said, "I want to give you something." I said, "All right, praise the Lord, I receive." He reached into his pocket and pulled out a check and handed it to me. He said, "Brother Price, the Lord told me last year to give you a certain amount of money." I never asked him for that money, but since I am a king, I am supposed to receive tribute. Of course, I have all the other things in my life in place. I am giving offerings, I am tithing, I am living upright, and doing everything I know to do based on God's Word.

The minister said, "This is the first installment on what the Lord told me to give you." The check was for $5,000. He said. "The Lord told me to give you $10,000." I said to him. "I believe every word of it." It had to be the Lord. It could not have been the devil!

When was the last time somebody gave you $5,000? Here is my point: Before I started confessing God's Word over my life, no one ever gave me $5.00, let alone $5,000! They did not give me anything except bills—a notice that they were about to repossess my car. And another notice telling me they were about to repossess my television set. I got those kinds of things. Nobody ever gave me $5,000. Today and for many years now, this kind of gift happens regularly because my wife and I are givers and claim our return on our giving based on God's Word.

Revelation 1:6:

> *and has made us kings and priests to His God and Father . . . .*

I am supposed to receive tribute and I claim my inheritance daily. I have taken God at His Word and it works!

I am a giver. I live to give. And I look forward to the day when I can give away a million dollars a shot, for the ministry, to help the Kingdom of God. As soon as I was given that $5,000, instantaneously my mind began to compute my tithe. I do that whenever I get anything. I do not think of how I can spend the money, but rather how much will the tithe be?

My heavenly Father said I should reign as a king in life. When I awake each morning, I look in the mirror and say, "Good morning, King Frederick, what is on the agenda for today? What new victories are we going to experience?"

CHAPTER THIRTEEN

FACT 4:

WHAT WE CAN DO IN CHRIST

The fourth biblical truth we must learn if we are to live victoriously in this life is "What We Can Do in Christ." This has to do with our empowering and our ability. You have ability through Jesus Christ in God, ability beyond your wildest dreams, beyond what tradition, in God, theology, and religious rituals have told you.

We have not been taught about our ability, yet the Bible is full of it. You can do everything that the Word of God says you can do. When you say what God's Word says, you are saying what God says. You are simply mimick-ing, or copying God Almighty.

More has been proclaimed from the pulpit about what we cannot do than about what we can do. They tell us we cannot do this, we cannot eat that, we cannot go there, we cannot comb our hair this way, we cannot, we cannot, we cannot! This is most of what we Christians have heard. This is not what the Word of God says.

Everything that the Word of God says you can do, you can do! However, you will never be able to do more than you are willing to confess that you can do, based upon God's revealed Weird. It is confession through faith that ignites and activates God's power in your life. We are not talking about saying positive things for the sake ot being positive. Being positive is better than being negative, but that is not what God is talking about. We are talking about the trigger that releases the bullet, the power ot God—His Words—our confession of His Words.

Proverbs 6:2:

> *You are snared by the words of your mouth;*
> *you are taken by the words of your mouth.*

This is a powerful scripture. A snare is a trap. So, in modern language, we could say it this way: You are trapped with the words of your mouth. If your words are words that limit you, then you will be limited. If your words are words that are contrary to what the Bible says about you, then you will be trapped by your negative confessions.

Now you can see the clever, insidious plot that Satan has contrived over the years to keep the Word ot God, the Bible, out of the hands of God's people. We must confess God's Word.

Philippians 4:13:

> *I can do all things through Christ who strengthens*
> *me.*

The *all things* are based upon what God says in His Word. I can do all things that God says I can do. I cannot just do all things, because as a man I cannot have a baby. I could say, "I am going to get pregnant," but that would be a dumb confession, which would not work.

Again, I can do all things through Christ who strengthens me, based on what God's Word declares, not just on some fantasy that you come up with out of the clear blue sky. "I can do all things through Christ" is the kind of mentality you have to develop, and you can develop that through the power of positive confession. It will change your environment in a positive way.

At first you may say, "This guy must be crazy. What is he talking about, words changing the environment?" Well, think about this, when a nation's leader declares we are at war, those words change your environment. Your whole scope of living changes just by the words of that individual.

When a man and woman stand before me as a minister, and I say, "Will you take this woman to be your wedded wife?" he could say, "No!" and he would stay in his same single environment. However, when he says, "Yes, I will," his life will change forever. His words changed his single environment to one of being married. If you start looking around, examining your whole life, everything eventually revolves back to something you got into by your words.

The virginity of some women was changed by their words. They did not know he was lying when he said, "I love you." He said he had never loved anyone as much as he loved you. Then he said, "Baby, if you really love me . . . ." and your virginity went out the window. He put his pants on, buttoned up his coat, slipped his belt around his waist, and said, "Bye-bye." Our words are powerful!

Even right now, many lives are a caldron of apparent hopelessness because way back in time somebody that you had a lot of confidence in, like a mother or a father, said, "You ain't no good, and you will never be any good. You are just like your old daddy. He was no good and you ain't gonna be nothin' either."

Sometimes, comments like these change people for the better, but most of the time, it changes them for the worse. Hateful words can crush the spirit. Words!

Let us examine some examples of your ability and your power in Christ.

Mark 16:17-18:

17 *"And these signs will follow those who believe:*
In My name they will cast out demons; they
will speak with new tongues;

18 *"they will take up serpents; and if they drink*
anything deadly, it will by no means hurt them;
they will lay hands on the sick, and they will
recover."

All of these things are positive. This is our ability in Christ, but we have to confess it and then follow that confession by action— doing it. This is why we do this at Crenshaw Christian Center, the church that I pastor. We lay hands on the sick. We cast out demons when it is necessary.

YOU MUST BELIEVE WHAT GOD SAYS IS TRUE

Some people say they do not believe in demons. This is fine. No problem. If you are smarter than God, I hope I can get to know you better. However, first I would like to see the universe that you have created, the one that you are sustaining by your power and might. When you say you do not believe in demons, you are saying that you are smarter than God, because God believes in demons. If God did not believe in demons, He would never give us authority to cast them out.

Demons must exist. They are the ones causing all this confusion going on in the world. They are the behind-the-scenes instigators of this confusion. Sometimes they have to be discerned and cast out.

Those that believe will speak with new tongues, cast out demons, take up serpents (accidentally), drink any deadly thing (unknown) and it will not hurt us. This is our authority and ability in Christ, but it will not work unless we confess and then do it.

John 14:12:

> *Most assuredly, I say to you, he who believes in*
> *Me, the works that I do he will do also; and*
> *greater works than these he will do, because I go*
> *to My Father.*

We should see the same works in the family of God that we see in the ministry of the Lord Jesus Christ. Yet, how many ministers tell you just the opposite of that, and have no scripture to back it up? The Church has swallowed that lie hook, line, sinker, the fishing pole, the reel, the fisherman and his boots! They say, "That went out with the early church. Miracles are not for today. This went out when the last apostle died."

Nowhere in the Bible will you find where it says those things went out when the last apostle died. All that is the rationale of man. Do you know why? Because they have not seen the works done. The assumption is that because we have not seen it done, then it is not for us today. It never occurred to them that maybe we are not doing our part in order to qualify for these things to be done.

Notice, Jesus said, *these signs will follow those who believe.* If you do not believe, the signs will not follow. It is not that you should just believe in Jesus, because there are many Christians who believe in Jesus, but they do not believe in the signs. Receiving Jesus as Savior and Lord is where we start, but you also have to believe in what He said.

These signs will follow those who believe: In My name they will cast out demons. You have to believe that you have the authority to do so. You have to believe that demons exist and believe you can cast them out when they get ugly and act up. They will speak with new tongues. However, you will not speak if you do not believe. They will lay hands on the sick, and they will recover. The qualification is that they cannot recover until hands are laid on them by those who believe.

The works that I do he will do also; and greater works than these he will do, because I go to My Father. We cannot do greater works in terms of quality, but we will do greater works in terms of quantity, because there are more of us than there were of Jesus. Understand that Jesus, at the time He walked the earth, was the only body on earth that was filled with the Holy Spirit. The Bible says that He had the Spirit without measure; therefore, as an individual person He would be able to do greater things than we would ever do as individuals.

Today, the Holy Spirit is not in me alone, but in every born-again, Spirit-filled believer. Each of us is only one infinitesimal part of the Body of Christ, so I can only do an infinitesimal part of what Jesus could do. Because when He walked the earth, He was the only Body of Christ that was filled with the Holy Spirit.

Jesus had all of the power working in Him, so He could do more things as an individual person than you or I could ever do individually. God has not limited His Spirit just to Fred Price. His Spirit is in the entire Body of Christ. Therefore, collectively, we can do greater works because there are more of us to do the work of the Lord. Greater in quantity, not greater in quality. After you have raised the dead that is a hard act to follow!

Think about this, Jesus had two hands and, at the very most, He could only lay hands on two people at the same time and get them healed. On the other hand, we are tens of thousands of hands. Therefore, it is conceivable that we could lay hands on tens of thousands of people at one time, when Jesus could only lay hands on two at a time. Therefore, we would be doing greater works quantitatively, but not qualitatively.

This is what we have; this is who we are; this is what we can do; and the key is we have to confess it and do it, if we want to experience it in our lives.

Matthew 17:20:

> So Jesus said to them, "Because of your unbelief; for assuredly, I say to you, if you have faith as a mustard seed, you will say to this mountain, 'Move from here to there,' and it will move; and nothing will be impossible for you.

Nothing will be impossible for you sounds like I can do all things through Christ, which adds up to the same thing. Now understand this, nothing will be impossible to you that God has said you can do. However, I have to believe that and confess it. I have to make it a part of my everyday life.

WE ARE OVERCOMERS

First John 5:4 says:

> For whatever [whoever] is born of God overcomes the world. And this is the victory that has overcome the world; our faith.

In the sight of our Father, we are overcomers. Right away, you can see that something is radically wrong among the ranks of Christianity. If we can overcome, then there should never be Christians getting divorces, because you have everything with which to win. "Well, she was not right for me," or, "he was not right for me." Wait a minute! You said the person was not right for you and that is why he or she is not. You can love anyone you want to love. Love is something you do. It is not automatic.

Marriage does not happen by itself. The Christians who know the Word and learn who they are in Christ; what they can do in Christ and confess those things can make a marriage work. Now, when I say make it work, I do not mean to tolerate and exist in a relationship that you hate every minute. What I am telling you is that you can get together and work it out, so that your spouse will be the best woman or man for you.

Do not tell me you cannot do it, because if you say you cannot do it, then that verse lied when it said, this is the victory that has overcome the world; our faith. By your faith, you can overcome a bad marriage. You can overcome anything that Satan has brought against you in your life. But you will have to believe it, and begin to confess it and then act in concert with it.

My Father is the One Who told me I am an overcomer. If I say I am not, then I am in contradiction to my Father. God cannot lie. If He says I can overcome the world, then I can overcome it. I may not be overcoming it, but that is not God's fault. It is my fault. Again, this is not a psyche job, this is the power of positive confession, this is what the Word says is yours. You have to see yourself as a victor. You have to see yourself overcoming, and then do not let any circumstance or any person tell you anything else, not even your wife or husband.

You are an overcomer. But you will have to fight. The Bible tells you, Fight the good fight of faith. You have to fight, and fighting is bloody, and fighting hurts, but we have already won the war in Jesus!

Say this out loud: "I am a world overcomer." Romans 10:17 says . . . *faith comes by hearing.* This is why you have to say it. This is what most Christians do not understand, and they will accuse you of bragging. However, when I confess the Word of God, I am not bragging. What I am doing is putting the law of God into operation. You see, if I want faith for the fact that I am a world-overcomer to come to me, I have to say it. Because the law says . . . *faith comes by hearing, and hearing by the word of God.*

When I say that I am a world-overcomer, I am speaking the Word of God, because the Word of God says . . . *this is the victory that has overcome the world – our faith.* When I first began confessing the Word, I could not beat a fly. Circumstances had me defeated. But I began saying it, "I am a world-overcomer!" I would go to bed at night and dream about overcoming the world. I would get up in the morning and say it again. I kept saying it until it became a part of me.

At first it was very imperceptible, but then all of a sudden, I woke up one morning and realized I had won some victories. It tasted so good! When you get to this place in faith you become bold, and you will not accept defeat from anyone. This is the power of positive confession!

First John 5:4 again:

> *For whatever* [or whoever] *is born of God overcomes the world. And this is the victory that has overcome the world – our faith.*

Who is he that overcomes the world? Fred Price. Put your name in there. He is talking about you. Who is he? Who is she? Who are they that overcome the world?

We found out from Proverbs 6:2 that you are trapped by the words of your mouth. Therefore, we need to be very careful about what we let come out of our mouths. Jesus said it like this in Matthew 12:37, *"For by your words you will be justified, and by your words you will be condemned."* By your words you are justified. Do you see how important your words are?

We can win through Jesus Christ. But you cannot do it passively. You cannot be a pacifist and win in this battle. You must believe, then you must confess what you believe and finally you must act on what you believe. Start now and you too will experience the blessings of God that come from *the power of positive confession.*

Apostle Frederick K.C. Price

Biography

Apostle Frederick K.C. Price is the founder of Crenshaw Christian Center (CCC) in Los Angeles, California. He began CCC in 1973, and shepherded it through 35 years into a ministry of world renown, with services held since 1989 in the 10,000-seat FaithDome.

In 1978, Apostle Price received instruction from God to begin a television broadcast. As a result, *Ever Increasing Faith Ministries* (EIFM) was launched, appearing initially in five of the nation's big-city television markets. Since that time, the broadcast has become global, and EIFM can be viewed on 132 stations in all 50 states and in six foreign countries. The broadcast is also heard on 15 radio programs and 19 Internet broadcast stations. Additionally, it can be seen on most social media platforms, including Facebook, Twitter, Instagram, YouTube, Pinterest, and others.

In 1990, Apostle Price founded the Fellowship of Inner-City Word of Faith Ministries (FICWFM), now renamed the Fellowship of International Christian Word of Faith Ministries. And in 2001, he established an East Coast church—Crenshaw Christian Center East.

A visionary and widely respected teacher, he is the author of some 50 books on faith, healing, prosperity, the Holy Spirit and other subjects. His book, *How Faith Works,* is a recognized classic on the operation of faith and its life-changing principles. He has also authored three historic volumes under the title of *Race, Religion & Racism.* Apostle Price has sold more than 2.1 million books since 1976. His most recent works include, *Prosperity: Good News for God's People* and *Answered Prayer Guaranteed: The Power of Praying with Faith.*

Although Apostle Price had already begun operating under the mantle of apostle, in 2008 he was publicly affirmed as an apostle of faith. Under his gift as teacher, he established several schools for ministry and formal education on the grounds of CCC. Among them are Frederick K.C. Price III Christian Schools (preschool to 12th grade); the Ministry

Training Institute; the CCC Correspondence School; the Frederick K.C. Price School of the Bible, and in 2008, the Apostle Price Ministry Training Center. Over the years, Apostle Price has received many prestigious awards—most notably, the Horatio Alger Award from the Horatio Alger Association of Distinguished Americans and the Southern Christian Leadership Council's Kelly Miller Smith Interfaith Award, both in 1978.

Apostle Price holds an honorary doctorate of divinity from Oral Roberts University in Tulsa, Oklahoma, and an honorary diploma from Rhema Bible Training Center in Broken Arrow, Oklahoma.

A year after his affirmation as apostle, and after more than 35 years as pastor, Apostle Price stepped aside to formally install his son, Frederick K. Price Jr., as pastor. He is currently the presiding prelate of CCC West and East, and serves at the helm as the chairman of CCC's board of directors. Apostle Price not only ministers in the FaithDome, but travels the world, mostly in the United States, teaching the uncompromising Word of God.

A devoted husband, Apostle Price has been married to Dr. Betty Price for 62 years. They are the proud parents of four children, and have 10 grandchildren, and four great-grandchildren.

Books by Apostle Frederick K.C. Price

HOW FAITH WORKS

RACE, RELIGION & RACISM, VOLUME 1
A Bold Encounter With Division in the Church

RACE, RELIGION & RACISM, VOLUME 2
Perverting the Gospel to Subjugate a People

RACE, RELIGION & RACISM, VOLUME 3
Jesus, Christianity and Islam

THE CHRISTIAN FAMILY
Practical Insight for Family Living

HOW TO OBTAIN STRONG FAITH
Six Principles

THE HOLY SPIRIT
The Helper We All Need

INTEGRITY
The Guarantee for Success

PROSPERITY
Good News for God's People

LIVING IN HOSTILE TERRITORY
A Survival Guide for the Overcoming Christian

ANSWERED PRAYER GUARANTEED

FAITH, FOOLISHNESS, OR PRESUMPTION?

IDENTIFIED WITH CHRIST:
A Complete Cycle From Defeat to Victory

DR. PRICE'S GOLDEN NUGGETS
A Treasury of Wisdom for Both Ministers and Laypeople

FIVE LITTLE FOXES OF FAITH

THE CHASTENING OF THE LORD

TESTING THE SPIRITS BEWARE!

THE LIES OF SATAN

*THE WAY, THE WALK,
AND THE WARFARE OF THE BELIEVER*
A Verse-by-Verse Study on the Book of Ephesians

THREE KEYS TO POSITIVE CONFESSION

THE PROMISED LAND
A New Era for the Body of Christ

A NEW LAW FOR A NEW PEOPLE

THE VICTORIOUS, OVERCOMING LIFE
A Verse-by-Verse Study on the Book of Colossians

PRACTICAL SUGGESTIONS FOR SUCCESSFUL MINISTRY

LIVING IN THE REALM OF THE SPIRIT

THE HOLY SPIRIT
The Missing Ingredient

IS HEALING FOR ALL?

GROWING IN GOD'S WORD:
Devotional & Prayer Journal

Minibooks

THE TRUTH ABOUT ... THE BIBLE

THE TRUTH ABOUT ... DEATH

THE TRUTH ABOUT ... DISASTERS

THE TRUTH ABOUT ... FATE

THE TRUTH ABOUT ... FEAR

THE TRUTH ABOUT ... HOMOSEXUALITY

THE TRUTH ABOUT ... RACE

THE TRUTH ABOUT ... WORRY THE

TRUTH ABOUT ... GIVING NOW FAITH IS

HOW TO BELIEVE GOD FOR A MATE

THANK GOD FOR EVERYTHING?

CONCERNING THOSE WHO HAVE FALLEN ASLEEP

THE ORIGIN OF SATAN

Specialty-size Books

WALKING IN GOD'S WORD
Through His Promises

WORDS OF WISDOM: WOW!

BUILDING ON A FIRM FOUNDATION

HOMOSEXUALITY:
State of Birth or State of Mind?

Spanish Language Books

COMO CREER EN DIOS PARA ENCONTRAR TU PAREJA

EDIFICANDONOS SOBRE UNA BASE FIRME
Una guia para el Desarrollo de Su Cristiana

To order books by Apostle Price, receive a book and disc catalog or be placed on the EIF mailing list, please call: **(800) 927-3436**

Books are also available at some local bookstores.

For more information, please write:

Crenshaw Christian Center

P.O. Box 90000

Los Angeles, CA 90009

or check your local TV listing:

Ever Increasing Faith Television Program

or visit our websites:

www.faithdome.org

www.faithdome.tv